THE
CONFESSIONS
OF AUGUSTINE
IN MODERN
ENGLISH

Other *Clarion Classics*

THE CONFESSIONS OF AUGUSTINE IN MODERN ENGLISH

Translated and Abridged by
SHERWOOD E. WIRT

 CLARION CLASSICS

Zondervan Publishing House
Grand Rapids, Michigan

CONTENTS

Preface to the Sixth Printing

It gives me much pleasure to introduce this latest printing of my translation of Augustine's *Confessions* to a special Upper Midwest readership. The other editions having gone the way of all printings, I am delighted to see the Doctor of Grace back in print—as I'm sure he is.

Over twenty years have passed since the original edition, *Love Song*, was issued by Harper & Row. My wife Winola, to whom it was dedicated, is now in heaven and presumably has met Augustine herself. I have remarried and would like to honor my wife Ruth with this edition.

Augustine is invariably represented in art as an aged saint with a white flowing beard. To read the *Confessions* is to discover a totally different kind of person. He is a real human being, full of faults and ambitious to reach the top, yet desperately eager to find God. In fifteen hundred years, no Christian has surpassed him in expressing his yearning and love for the Divine.

May this rendition of an ancient classic stir your own heart, and inspire you to greater heights in serving the Lord in this generation.

Sherwood Eliot Wirt
April 1991

INTRODUCTION

A translation is no translation, he said,
unless it will give you the music of a
poem along with the words of it.
          J. M. SYNGE, *The Aran Islands*

Why Augustine? Why would an American journalist undertake
to translate from the Latin something written 1,500 years ago by
a Catholic bishop—in Africa? Especially when the journalist is
engaged in nonpartisan evangelistic work? The reason is that I
love him. Or can't you say that any more? I am saying it because
he has done a beautiful thing in my life. He has shared his struggles
and his search for God with me (and with millions like me) and
has done it without sacrificing a first-class intellect, without trying
to polish his image, and without stooping to religious clichés.

During the year that I lived with this brilliant young teacher of
rhetoric, I shared the terrors of his childhood, the wildness of his
adolescence, the frustrations of his early manhood, the develop-
ment of his astonishing mental powers. I reveled in his honesty,
although it left me wondering if I could ever write as open an
autobiography. I joined him in the tough, unrelenting search for
truth and reality. I saw him stand like Job and assault the citadel
of divine mystery: "Where did the devil's evil will come from?
Didn't the Creator, who is all good, make his angels all good?"
I stayed with him all the way through the boulders and rapids and
white water, until we came at last into the calm, majestic current
of authentic Christian faith. The excitement and exhilaration I
felt while working through Books 7 and 8 of the *Confessions* come
back each time I leaf through the pages.

A passion to bring Augustine to our generation grew out of my editorial chores on *Decision* magazine. It became evident that a language barrier was depriving millions of modern readers of the inspiration of great Christian literature. Many translations of the classics seem to me, in fact, to be more archaic than the original. The corpus of faith gathered through the centuries is ignored because people find the ancients impossible to read.

For thirty years I had heard that the *Confessions* was a great book, but each time I tried to tackle the English text it proved too much for me. I decided my dull wit was keeping me from appreciating good literature. Now I know better. The translations are not good literature; the book's lasting fame is based on its original form. When in December, 1969, I sat to the actual task of translating, I found that the Latin in which Augustine wrote was superb. Its smoothly flowing rhetoric abounded in word play, and was at times racy, at times intricate, but always vivid and eloquent. No wonder the late Professor Gibb could write, "Alone of all the writings of the fathers of the church, the *Confessions* belong to the literature of the whole world, having been read in the original . . . more than any other Latin book with the exception of Vergil."

Then what about the translations? For our work has been rendered, in Gibb's words, "into the speech of every cultivated people." Today the *Confessions* remains a book to which the English-speaking world tips its hat, but which nobody reads. Let me gratefully acknowledge the help I have received from the seven English translations with which I have been working closely. While extending every deserved honor to these scholars for their achievement, and while acknowledging that the newer translations are becoming more readable, I maintain a friendly controversy with them. I feel we are given the letter of Augustine but not always the spirit. In their fidelity to the text, our translators have sometimes thrown up an academic smokescreen which it is my hope to dissipate. For the Bishop of Hippo wrote not as an academic or a scholar, but as a lover. His *Confessions* is not a textbook but a love song.

A question could be raised about my own qualifications as a translator, since I have admitted to being no scholar. What right have I to invade this field? I stand awestruck, in fact, on the fringe of a vast field of research that has pre-empted some of the finest minds of the church for a millennium and a half. Volumes have been written about every conceivable aspect of the *Confessions*, including its punctuation. The doctors of the Augustinian order (which Augustine founded) have led the way in collecting and collating the various manuscripts. With Christians everywhere I join in thanksgiving for all this labor of love, and would like to render tribute for all the devoted, painstaking effort it has taken to produce a readable and accurate Latin text.

If I have any excuse for entering the field, it is because I want the blessing I have received from these writings to be shared by many others. Perhaps this could be called a "coffee-break" translation—Augustine for the ordinary man and woman. I take courage from a comment made to me by Dr. Calvin Linton of George Washington University (its original source, I believe, is John Dryden) to the effect that a translator's best asset is his familiarity not with another language, but with his own. To master the rudiments of another tongue is not difficult when a common alphabet is used, but to master the nuances of one's own native language, and to use it simply and clearly to express one's meaning, calls for the skill of a lifetime.

Basic translation work consists of a multitude of small decisions, but occasionally the translator is required to establish a policy of style. In this book I have taken certain liberties that require explanation. Augustine's references to the Manichean religion, in which he was more or less involved for a dozen years, have been trimmed to a minimum. His interest seems to have been more philosophical than religious, and in any case the Manichean system holds little interest for us today. None of the books of its founder, Mani, is extant, but some idea of his teachings may be gained from any standard encyclopedia (see p. 39).

The word "Catholic" appears in one form or another perhaps a dozen times in the Latin text of the *Confessions*. In this translation I have chosen at times to render it in its generic sense of "whole" or "universal," while at other times I have omitted it. The decision not to use the expression "Catholic church," which Augustine employs on rare occasions in the *Confessions*, was prompted in part by the religious situation of our own day. We often find Roman Catholics, Greek Catholics, Armenian Catholics, and Anglo-Catholics referring to the "Catholic church" in a more restrictive sense, I would say, than the term held for the Mediterranean world of the fourth century. With all deference to and veneration for the distinguished Augustinian tradition in the Roman Catholic church, I am convinced that the simple word "church" comes closer today to rendering what Augustine himself sought to convey. Many things could be said about the views Augustine set forth or did not set forth in these pages regarding the church, but it is best to let him speak for himself.

The *Confessions* of Augustine is one of his three major works, and thanks to his early training in rhetoric, it ranks with the finest of ancient literature. It was composed between A.D. 398 and 400, perhaps fourteen years after Augustine's conversion. He was in his early forties. The first nine books are autobiographical, and the last three (11-13) form an extended Bible interpretation based on Genesis 1. The tenth book is an assessment of the state of his Christian faith at the time of writing. Following the precedent of certain earlier translators, I have limited the present rendering to the first ten books. From Books 9 and 10 I have extracted only certain immortal passages, for the first eight books really tell the story. I have not hesitated, in meeting the requirements of this edition, occasionally to eliminate obscure references. There has also been an effort to deal with repetitiveness in order to present a unified book in briefer compass.

Some of the later passages dealing with Augustine's mother, Monnica, whose influence on her son principally through her prayer life is well known, have been omitted. The famous scene at Ostia just prior to her death is one of the most moving portions of the *Confessions*, but since it comes after his conversion experience I have chosen not to include it.

Finally there is a disagreement between my view of the experience in the garden at Milan and that held by a few Augustinian scholars. Some authorities I have read appear to contend that Augustine was already an (unbaptized) Christian when he came to his moment of decision, and that the only issue at stake when he flung himself under the fig tree was the direction of his personal sex life. I cannot accept such a view because I do not believe Augustine held it. To him the issue was, Did he belong to God or did he not? Until his will was captured and wholly committed, he did not consider that he was God's. One conclusion he drew from his garden experience, to be sure, was that he should not take a wife. Yet there was no call to the priesthood here. I feel strongly that the issue was a larger one than mere asceticism, and bore upon the total alignment of his life—not so much what he would *do* as what he would *be*—thereby touching upon regeneration itself, and the universal evangelistic appeal of the gospel. I have consequently left out of this translation the reference to not taking a wife (Book 8, Section 12) in order that the reader may grasp some of the other and more important elements that were involved in this basic transaction between a man and his God.

I come back to the original question: "Why Augustine?" Perhaps some words by Fathers Campbell and McGuire in their study of the *Confessions* express it better than I can:

> The importance of Augustine to the story of civilization
> is not to be easily exaggerated. His name is the last in point
> of time of the great names of antiquity; in influence on
> the thought of after-ages his name is one of the first. He

was not the most learned of the Latin fathers . . . yet in sheer greatness of stature he towers above them all. . . .

[He had] an Athenian elasticity and freedom [that] seized the meaning of Christianity with an insight which has never been surpassed. . . . Because he surpassed all ancient thinkers, save Plato and Aristotle, in philosophic power, he surpassed all other fathers in philosophic appreciation of Christianity. . . . Out of his *Confessions* came a type of literature unknown to the world before.

To which Outler's comment may be added: "He was far and away the best—if not the very first—psychologist in the ancient world."

Augustine was born in Thagaste, North Africa, in A.D. 354. His mother has been celebrated for centuries as St. Monnica, but the *Confessions* does not picture her as saintly in her early years. His father was a pagan who was baptized just before his death. After showing brilliance in schooling, Augustine was sent to Carthage for further training and became a teacher of rhetoric. In 383 he went to Rome to improve his situation, and eventually became a teacher in Milan. What happened in Milan is told in these pages. Returning to North Africa to live an informal life as a Christian recluse, Augustine was elected priest by acclamation while on a visit to the church in Hippo, and subsequently was named bishop in 396.

For the next thirty-four years until his death he engaged in extensive writing, along with the arduous duties of his diocese. Much of what he wrote was polemical; the imminent collapse of Rome heightened the significance of his defense of the faith. When he died in 430 the Vandals were besieging the gates of Hippo, and they captured it the following year.

Three major critical editions of the Latin text of the *Confessions* are available. I have translated selections from only one of them, the second edition of the text edited by Gibb and Montgomery and published by Cambridge in 1927. The English translations to which I have referred for assistance are: Edward Bouverie Pusey,

London, 1838; J. G. Pilkington, London, 1876; F. J. Sheed, Sheed & Ward, New York, 1943; Albert C. Outler, Library of Christian Classics, Westminster, Philadelphia, 1955; John K. Ryan, Image Books, Doubleday, Garden City, 1960; R. S. Pine-Coffin, Penguin Books, Baltimore, 1961; Rex Warner, Mentor-Omega, New American Library, New York, 1963.

I have also profited from studying the Latin text of the *Confessions*, edited by James M. Campbell and Martin R. P. McGuire (Prentice-Hall, 1930). The biography *St. Augustine* by the French author Jacques Chabannes (Doubleday, 1962) is one of the best available in English. *St. Augustine's Confessions, the Odyssey of a Soul*, by Robert J. O'Connell (Harvard University Press, 1969) and *The Christian Philosophy of St. Augustine*, by Etienne Gilson (Random House, 1960) are useful psychological and philosophical studies of the man. For sheer enjoyment I commend *St. Augustine and His Influence Through the Ages*, by Henri Marrou, translated by Patrick Hepburne-Scott (Longmans, Green and Co. Ltd., 1957).

It was in 1942 that I first became acquainted with Aurelius Augustinus during a student seminar at the Pacific School of Religion. I learned that he wrote at a time when Rome, which had ruled Western civilization for a thousand years, was crumbling in ruins. The empire was being cut to pieces by destructive rival armies. Barbarians stormed through the gates of the "eternal city" because the young Romans were saying, in so many words, "Hell, no, we won't go." * Yet at the moment when men were unleashing the force that would bury a civilization in its own rubble, this quiet account of a soul's quest for God was being written.

Who knows or cares today about what happened along the shores of the Great Sea in the fourth and fifth centuries? But we have this book. It is the durable, honest witness of a man to whom Christians of every age and persuasion owe an incalculable debt.

---

* "One had to speak German in order to understand the last defenders of Rome" (Jean Duché, *Histoire du Monde*, quoted in Chabannes, *St. Augustine*, p. 230).

In particular, students of the Reformation should realize how freely Luther (himself once an Augustinian monk), Calvin, Zwingli and the other sixteenth-century Reformers drew upon these and other writings of the "Doctor of Grace" in their drive to recover the authority and supremacy of Scripture.

May I express my thanks to my colleagues on the staff of *Decision* magazine for their help in the preparation of this volume, and to the libraries of the University of Minnesota and Bethel College, as well as the Minneapolis Public Library, for assistance. To Miss Kersten Beckstrom goes a special word of sincere gratitude for her expert preparation of the typescript. The book would never have been completed without her assistance.

S. E. W.

Minneapolis, Minnesota
October, 1970

BOOK ONE

Infancy and Childhood

1

How great you are, Lord, and how greatly to be praised! [1] How matchless is your power and how infinite your understanding. [2] Man may be but a speck in your wide creation, but he wants to praise you. He may carry around with him his mortality and his sin as mute testimony to the truth that "God resists the proud," [3] but even so he wants to praise you. You have thrilled us by causing us to delight in your praise. You have made us for yourself, and our hearts are restless till they find their rest in you. [4]

I need to know, Lord, which properly comes first: Should I call on you for help or should I praise you? Is it important to know you first before I call on you? If I don't know who you are, how can I call? In my ignorance I might be calling on some other object of worship. Do I call on you, then, in order to know you? "But how are men to call upon him in whom they have not believed? . . . And how are they to hear without a preacher?" [5] The Psalmist says, "Those who seek him shall praise the Lord!" [6] It means those who seek him shall find him, and when they have found him, they will praise him. So it's settled; let me seek you, Lord, by asking for your help in my life. I will call on you, believing in you, for you certainly have been preached to us. I will call in the faith you gave me, Lord, that you inspired in me through

the assuming of human nature by your Son, and through the min-
istry of his preacher.*

2

But wait. How can I call upon my Lord and my God, since
when I call, I am calling him to myself? What room is there in me
for God—the God who made the universe? What capacity do I
have for containing you, Lord? Do heaven and earth contain you?
I know that nothing can exist without you; does that mean that
whatever exists contains you? I also exist; and if I couldn't exist
unless you were in me, why do I keep asking you to enter into me?
Even if I were in hell—which I am not—you would be there. "If
I make my bed in hell, behold, thou art there." [7] I simply couldn't
live at all, my God, unless you were in me; or rather, unless I were
in you, by whom, of whom, and in whom are all things. Lord,
that's the way it is. To what place shall I call you, then, since I am
in you? From which direction will you come to me? Can I travel
past the boundary of the universe so that my God might come to
me—he who has said, "Do I not fill heaven and earth?" [8]

3

Let me go on: Do the heavens and the earth contain you, since
you fill them? Or do you cram them to overflowing, since they
cannot contain you? And if you do overflow the universe, into what
do you overflow? Is it that you contain all things, and so have no
need for anything to contain you, because you fill them simply by

* Augustine is referring to Bishop Ambrose, whom he heard in Milan in
A.D. 386, and whose preaching was instrumental in his conversion (see Book
6, Section 3).

containing them? The vessels you fill won't hold you; and yet if they were to be smashed, you would not be spilt. But if you did pour yourself down upon us, there would be no waste—we would be buoyed up. You would not be scattered or dissipated, but would gather us together. And then, when you fill all things, do you do it with your whole Being? Since all things cannot wholly contain you, does that mean that they contain part of you? Do they contain the same part, or do different parts of the universe contain different parts of you—greater parts or lesser according to their capacity? Are some parts of you greater and some lesser? Or are you everywhere, even though nothing contains you wholly?

4

Who are you, really? Who if not the Lord God? "For who is God, but the Lord?" [9] You are the acme, the pinnacle of everything: of goodness, power, mercy, justice, beauty and strength; of hiddenness and nearness; of stability and mystery. You are unchanging and yet you change everything. You are never new, never old; yet you make all things new. You humiliate the proud without their knowing it. You are always active, always resting; gathering, yet needing nothing; bearing, filling, protecting, creating, nourishing, perfecting, seeking what you don't need. You love without getting involved in passion. You are jealous, yet you remain unconcerned. You repent, but without being sorry. You become angry, yet you stay serene. You change your operations but never your plans. You recover what you did not lose in the first place. Never in want, you rejoice at what you have won. Never greedy, you exact regular interest. Men will spend their last dime to get you under obligation to them; yet who has anything that is not yours to begin with? You pay debts where you owe nothing, and when you forgive debts you lose nothing.

4

But what have I really been saying, my God, my life, my delight? What can anyone say about you? Those who talk the most are no better than those who say nothing—yet to keep silence about you is equally dangerous!

5

Who will give me what it takes to rest in you? Who will make it so you come into my heart and captivate it, so I can forget my rottenness and take hold of you, the one good thing in my life? What are you to me? Be lenient with me, Lord, so I can talk to you. What am I to you, that you should order me to love you, and then become angry and hold all kinds of threats over me if I don't? Suppose I don't love you, is it all that important? Woe is me! Perhaps you had better tell me straight out, O Lord my God, just what you are to me. Say to my soul, "I am your salvation." [10] Speak so I can hear you. Take a good look, Lord, my heart is right here listening. Reveal yourself and say to my soul, "I am your salvation." I will come running after that voice and lay hold on you. Don't hide your face from me; let me see it even though I die, for I shall surely die if I don't see it.

The house of my soul is too small to let you in; you will have to expand it. It lies in ruins; you will have to rebuild it. There are things in it, I know and confess, that are offensive to your sight. But who will clean it up? To whom else besides you can I cry out, "Clear me from my hidden faults. Keep back thy servant also from presumptuous sins"? [11] I believe, therefore I speak: Lord, you know how it is.[12] Have I not confessed openly my wrongdoing? And you, my God, have forgiven the guilt of my heart! [13]

I will not fight against your justice, since you are truth itself, and I have no intention of putting myself in a false position by letting my sins trip me up. That is why I refuse to contend in judgment with you: because if you were to mark iniquity, Lord, Lord, who could stand? [14]

6

Yet I ask to be allowed to speak in the presence of your mercy. I, who am dust and ashes, ask to speak since it is to your mercy that I address myself, and not to a man who would laugh at me for doing it. You could scorn me too, if you wanted to; but instead you turn and have compassion on me.

What I want to say, Lord, is that I don't know where I came from, when I came into this living death. Or should I call it death in life? I don't know. Yet the gifts your mercy provides have borne me up from the very beginning—not that I remember that far back, but I have heard about it from my natural parents, by whom and in whom you first made me a being in time. When human milk was fed me for my sustenance, it was not my mother's breasts that filled me, but you yourself who disposed that I should be provided with infant food—since your bounty operates on every level of the universe. You arranged for me to want no more than you provided, and for others to give me what I needed. They did it with instinctive affection out of the abundance you had given. It was good for them to do good to me, even though the good came really not *from* them but *through* them. You, God, are the source of all good things; from my God is all my health.[15] That is what I have since discovered, and you have made it abundantly clear by what I have seen you give both to me and to those about me. But at the time of infancy I knew how to suckle, how to lie quietly when content, and how to cry when in pain. That was about all.

Afterward I began to laugh, first in my sleep and then when awake—or so I have been told.[16] I believe it even though I don't remember it, because I have observed the same thing in other infants. Gradually I came to realize where I was, and tried to make my wishes known to those who could satisfy them, but I could not. My wants were inside me, and those around me were "outside," so to speak; there was no way they could come into my inner life. So I would fling my arms and kick my legs and use my voice, making the few signs I could but not to any great effect. And when I didn't get what I wanted because it wasn't good for me, or because I had failed to communicate, I became indignant and took my revenge in crying. I treated my elders as though they were slaves—even those upon whom I had no claim. Such, I have since noticed, is the way of infant behavior; and I have learned more about myself by watching other infants than from the nurses who knew me at that age.

My infancy passed from the scene a long time ago, but I am still around. Now, Lord, there's something I would like to ask you. I know you live forever, and nothing that is in you dies. I know you are God and Lord of all you have created, and you existed before time and even before whatever it is that can be called "before." With you there is stability in the midst of the precarious, changelessness in the midst of change, reason in the midst of confusion. But speak to your unworthy petitioner now, and tell me whether I existed in any earlier state than my infancy. What about the time I spent in my mother's womb? I have observed pregnant women and have learned something about the prenatal condition; but what was I even before that, my God, my joy? Was I anywhere? Was I anyone? No one seems to be able to tell me. I couldn't find out from my father or mother, or out of the experience of others, or even from my own memory. Are you laughing at me for asking such a thing? Are you telling me to be content to praise and confess you for the things that I do know?

I do praise you, Lord of heaven and earth, for bringing me into existence, and for my infancy of which I remember nothing. You seem to have left man to learn about himself from others, and to accept much of what he knows on the authority of women! In any case I had life and being, and toward the end of infancy I began to look for signs by which I could let others know what I wanted.

Where could such an animal have come from, Lord, except from you? Can anybody create himself? Is there any other source from which life and being could flow into us, except from you? You made us, Lord, and life and being are undivided in you, for you are yourself Eternal Life and Infinite Being. You who are supreme are also unchanging, yet in you the present moment is never lost and never passes away. In another sense, of course, it does pass away, because you control everything, and there would not even be anything to change unless you upheld it in the first place. And since your years have no end,[17] your years make up an Everlasting Day. How many of our days, as well as our fathers', have passed through that Everlasting Day of yours, and have received from it their measure and manner of being! So it shall be in the days to come, and still you are the same.[18] All our yesterdays from the beginning of time, and all our tomorrows to the end of time, come from this your Day.

What is it to me if somebody fails to understand this? Let him be happy who is able to ask, "What is it all about?" Let him celebrate the fact that *he wants to love you*, even if he fails to find the answer to life—how much better that is than to look for the answer and miss out on finding you!

7

"Hear me, God. What a mess man's sin has made!" When a man begins to talk that way, it's a sign of your mercy on him, Lord, because you made man and not the sin in him.

Who remembers the sins of my infancy? In your sight nobody is without sin, not even the child that has lived but one day on earth.[19] But who will recapture my past? Perhaps each baby in whom I see what can no longer be remembered about myself. What were my sins? Did I bawl too loudly for the breast? Were I to do so now (not for the breast, but, say, for adult food) I would be ridiculed and reprimanded. What I did then probably deserved a scolding, too, but since I couldn't understand the meaning of correction at that age, neither custom nor common sense condemned me.

As we grow older we reject such behavior; yet I have never seen a man knowingly prune away the good along with the evil. Even as a tiny baby it was not exactly a good idea for me to try to get something by screaming when it would have been harmful to me; or to become furious at those elders who would not indulge me, and to strike out at them, with intent to hurt, because they didn't give in to my demands which could only have done me mischief. Obviously the innocence of the baby lies in the helplessness of its body rather than in the state of its mind. I have seen a baby turn pale with jealousy as it watched another infant at the breast. This is not unusual. Mothers and nurses tell me that they have their own remedies for driving out fits of jealousy. But can you call it "innocence" when a child demands that milk be withheld from another child who would die without it, when there is plenty to go around? We look tolerantly on such behavior, not because it's acceptable, but because we know it will eventually be outgrown. That it's a serious matter can be proved from the fact that we won't put up with such conduct when we detect it in an older person.

My Lord and my God, you gave me life in my infancy, you endowed me with senses, you shaped my body with limbs and beautified it with form; and for its well-being and security you supplied it with all the vital impulses needed by a living being. You have commanded me to glorify you for these things, to confess you and to sing praises to your name, O Most High.[20] Even if you had done nothing else but this, which nobody else but you can do, you are God, the One, omnipotent and good, most beautiful of all, the measure of reality, who formed the universe and ordained it according to your law.

Lord, I don't care to dwell any longer on this part of my life, which lies outside my memory, and about which I must take the word of others and conjecture what I can from observing children. Like the time I spent in my mother's womb, it is lost forever in the darkness of oblivion. If it be true that I was brought forth in iniquity, and that in sin did my mother conceive me,[21] where, I ask you, my God, where, Lord, or when was I, your servant, ever innocent? But now I pass by that time of life; for what more can I say about a period of which I cannot recall the slightest trace?

8

From infancy I grew into boyhood, or rather, it grew into me. My early years did not "go away" (where would they go?), they simply didn't exist any more. I was no longer an infant unable to talk, but a boy equipped with the gift of speech. This I remember, and since then I have found out by observation how I first learned to speak. My elders did not teach me in any systematic way as they later taught me my letters. I used the mind that you, my God, had given me, and with an assortment of grunts and whimperings and movements of my arms and legs, made my point. I have thought out the matter with the aid of memory in this way: When my elders made some particular sound, and at the same time pointed to something, I realized that the thing they pointed to was called by the sound they were using.

What they meant was made plain by the motions of their bodies, using a kind of natural language common to folk everywhere, with changes of expression, eye movements, gestures, and tones of voice—all calculated to express a mental attitude toward something, whether it was to be sought after, held, thrown away, or otherwise avoided. So as I kept hearing words repeated in various contexts I gradually identified the objects that they stood for, and teaching myself to enunciate the same sounds, I was able to express my will. By the use of verbal signs I learned to communicate with those about me, and so climbed a little higher in the stormy life of human society, still dependent on the authority of my parents and subject to the will of my elders.

9

God, my God, what a dog's life I was forced to undergo during my boyhood, after it was pressed on me as my duty that I must obey my teachers. It seemed that there was no other way to get on in the world and excel in language skills, and so gain honor among men and acquire deceitful riches for myself. So I was packed off to school without understanding the reason for it, fool that I was, and if I proved slow at grasping the teaching, they whipped me.[22] That was the way our ancestors had always done it, and so many others have followed that course since, making a track of multiplied misery and toil for the sons of Adam.

At that time, Lord, we found men praying to you; and we learned from them, as we were able, to think of you as some great being who (though we could not see you) was able to hear us and help us. So as a boy I too began praying to you, my help and my refuge,[23] and in calling on you, broke the strings that bound my tongue. I begged—small as I was but with no small show of energy—that I might not be whipped at school. And while you would not listen to my foolishness, the grownups around me (and even my parents, who certainly wished me no ill) simply laughed at my welts and bruises, which were anything but a joke to me.

Has there ever been anyone, Lord, with such a noble spirit, who was so close to you and so in love with you (or who was so stupid) that he could rise to a sublime height from which he could look complacently on the racks and claws and other torture instruments that men all over the world fervently pray to be allowed to escape? Then how could our parents be amused by the torments with which the teachers punished us boys? To us the punishments were just as frightening, and called forth just as much earnest praying, as if we had been grown up. But in spite of our terror, we kept right on with our misbehavior by failing to complete our reading, writing, and study assignments. We were not deficient, Lord, in either memory or ability; thanks to your provision, we had enough to meet our age requirements. But our great love was playing at sports, and for this we were punished by grown men who were doing exactly the same thing themselves. They like to call their playing around "business"; but when boys play around they are promptly slapped down by their elders, and no one feels sorry for them any more than they would for the men.

Let me ask this: Would any reasonable person approve of my being whipped as a boy for playing ball, because it hindered my studies and kept me from mastering the arts of reading and writing, when those same studies would only prepare me to play as a grownup at more discreditable games? Look at the teacher who took it upon himself to beat me. Was he any better than I? When he got the worst of some little squabble with a fellow teacher, I noticed he was far more upset than I was when I lost a match to a better ballplayer.

10

And yet I did wrong, Lord my God—ruler and creator of everything in nature (but not the creator of sin)—I did wrong in acting contrary to the precepts of my parents and those same teachers. The lessons they tried to force me to learn, from whatever motives, would have helped me later on. I disobeyed not because I had something better to do, but from sheer love of play. I reveled in the glow of an athletic victory. I was intrigued, too, by the dramatic fictions of the stage, which tickled my ears and made them itch the more;

while my eyes fairly bugged out at the spectacles and games put on by the grownups.* Yet I notice that those who stage such enter-tainments are highly regarded by the general public, most of whom would be pleased if their children followed some such career. Most people would agree, too, that their children should be whipped if the games they played interfered with their studies, for schoolwork is the means by which a child may go after and achieve such a distinguished career! Look at us, Lord. Have mercy on us, and un-shackle those of us who call on you. Do more than that! Unbind those who never stopped to ask you for a thing, just so they might learn to call on you, and so find themselves set free at last.

11

I had heard as a boy about the eternal life that was promised to us through the Lord our God, who had humbled himself and de-scended to us in our pride. In fact, as soon as my mother had delivered me, because of her great faith in you, I was sealed with the mark of his cross, and periodically thereafter was sprinkled with the sacred salt. You saw, Lord, that as a boy I was suddenly seized with stomach cramps one day, and nearly died. You also saw, my God (because even then you were my Guardian), how strong were my feelings and my faith when I pleaded with my mother and the Mother of us all, your church,[24] for the baptism of your Christ, my Lord and my God. This greatly disturbed my own mother, who with her pure and faithful heart had given a great deal of care and pains to the matter of my eternal salvation. Had I not quickly re-covered, I would have received the sacrament of baptism, and would have confessed you, Lord Jesus, and so known the forgiveness of sins.[25]

But my spiritual renewal was postponed, it being reasoned that

* Every Mediterranean city in Roman times had its amphitheater where gladiatorial and other "games" provided popular amusement.

if I did live, I would only get myself into a worse mess, and it would be more dangerous to my soul if I had been baptized, because the guilt for sin would then be the greater. I ask you, my God, and would like to know if you are willing to tell me, what the point was in postponing my baptism. Was it a good idea to let the reins go slack, so that I might sin all the more? Or weren't the reins really all that slack?

Why do we constantly have it drummed into our ears, "Let him alone, let him do as he pleases, he is not yet baptized"? They don't say that about physical health. No one advises, "Let him alone, let him hurt himself some more, he is not yet healed." I say it would have been far better if I had been made whole right then, so that I could have used the help of my friends and my own efforts to place my soul's restored health in your keeping, who gave it to me in the first place. Much better! Many and mighty were the waves of temptation that threatened to break over me as I grew out of boyhood. My mother was aware of them, but decided it would be better to expose the unmolded clay rather than clay in which the image of Christ had been formed.

1 2

In this time of boyhood, which was fraught with less peril than my later adolescence, I disliked my studies and hated being driven to them. But I was driven, and benefited as a result, though I can take no credit for it, for had it been my way I would have learned nothing at all. No man does well when he is going against his own will, even if what he is doing is good. As for those who urged me to study, they deserve no credit either; for the benefits I received came from you, my God. They could not have cared less about the way I would later put to use what they were forcing me to learn; what they taught me simply intended to sate the insatiable—that is, to fulfill the desire of men for hollow wealth and ignominious glory.

But you, Lord, who have numbered the hairs of our heads, used for my benefit the mistaken motivation of those who were egging me on at my studies, and you used my own error in not being willing to learn to punish me. That punishment was not entirely inappropriate for such a small boy who was such a great sinner. Thus you did well by me even though you had to use those who were doing the opposite; and as for my sins, you gave me just retribution. Evidently you have ordained that every disorder of the soul becomes its own punishment.

13

Why is it that ever since boyhood I have found the study of Greek literature so obnoxious? I still don't know. I have always loved Latin—not just the grammar but also the literature we were taught later. But those first lessons in reading, writing, and arithmetic were just as hard and repugnant in their way as the Greek was. Here, you might say, can be found good evidence of sin and the vanity of human weakness; for I was but "flesh; a wind that passeth away, and cometh not again." [26] And yet those early lessons were certainly better than the later ones, for they taught me what I still retain—the power to read what is written and to write what I wish to express. But in other studies I was forced to learn about the wayward meanderings of a character named Aeneas [27]—all the time overlooking my own waywardness; and to shed tears over the corpse of Queen Dido of Carthage, who is supposed to have killed herself for love of this man. But all the while I was quite dry-eyed, my living God, about the way these studies were causing my own pitiful self to become dead toward you.

Here is the most miserable of all men: one who would sob over the death of somebody like Dido, who supposedly suffered through her love of Aeneas; yet he did not shed one tear over his own suffering, brought on by his failure to love you, God, Light of my heart,

Bread who feeds my inner soul, Power who joins my mind to the thoughts of my heart. I did not love you, so I went whoring from you; [28] and in my whoring I heard the shouts all about me: "Bravo! Bravo!" [29] For the friendship of this world is fornication against you; [30] yet the cry, "Bravo!" is echoed so loudly that one is ashamed to be any other kind of man.

For all this I did not weep, but for Dido I did, because she killed herself, "seeking by the sword a stroke and wound extreme." I too became an extremist, on the prowl for the rottenest things in your creation. When I deserted you it was a case of earth sinking back to earth. If for some reason I was not permitted to read, then I would become upset over not being able to read what upset me! And this was the kind of demented stuff that was considered more honorable and fruitful than the studies that taught us how to read and write.

But now, my God, kick up a mighty clamor in my soul. Let your truth tell me straight out, "It isn't so! It isn't so! The first study was far better!" Speaking for myself, rather than forget how to write and read, I would vastly prefer to forget all about the aimless wanderings of Aeneas and his crew. Let those who would protest my attitude hold their tongues; I fear them no longer. To you, my God, I confess what my soul really longs for: the inner peace that will enable me to restrain my evil ways, so I can learn to choose your good ways.

Let those who buy and sell books likewise shut their mouths. Were I to ask them whether it be true, as the poet claims, that Aeneas once came to Carthage, the ignoramuses among them would probably admit they didn't know, while the more educated would say flat out that he did not. Yet if I were to ask how the name Aeneas was spelled, every last one who had gone to school would answer correctly, according to the conventional use of the alphabet.

Let's put it another way: If I were to ask which would be the greater loss to society, the disappearance of reading and writing skills or the disappearance of such figments of poetic imagination, isn't it plain to anyone whose mind has not gone blank what the answer would be? My mistake as a boy was in preferring the inane over the useful; or more accurately, in loving the one and hating the other. "One plus one makes two; two plus two equals four"—I found that kind of chanting repulsive. But the wooden horse full of armed troops, and the burning of Troy, and the appearance of Creusa's ghost—these were the spectacles that delighted my vanity.

14

If my Greek studies contained such tales—and they did—why did I hate them so? I imagine that when schoolboys in Greece are forced to study Vergil's Latin, they hate it as much as I did Homer's Greek. I did not know one word of the language; but to make me learn, my vehement masters pressured me with all kinds of terrifying threatenings and punishments.

When I was an infant, of course, I had no knowledge of Latin either, but managed to learn it without dread or torture simply by directing my attention to the pleasantries of my nurses, the laughter of those around me, and the words of delight of those who played with me. I learned it all without being pushed by threat of punishment, for my own heart led me to express what was in my mind—a thing impossible unless I had found a way to use the language. I learned not from those who taught me, but from those who talked with me, as I tried to pour into their ears the way I felt about things.

From all this it is plain enough that a free curiosity is more effective in learning than a rigid discipline. Yet by your law the free flow has to be controlled, God; by your law (whether it be the schoolmaster's stick or the testings of the martyrs) we are called back to you, through a mixture of the wholesome and the bitter, from the destructive delights that once pulled us away from you.

15

Lord, I implore you, don't let my soul come apart under your discipline. Don't let me forget to confess the mercy you have shown me in rescuing me from all my evil ways. You I find to be lovelier than all the seductions I ever went after. I love you with all my strength, and I take hold of your hand with my whole heart, so that you might snatch me away from every temptation right to the end. Take notice, Lord, my King and my God: I am offering you everything useful I learned as a boy, and everything I now speak and write and read and compute. When I was learning a lot of worthless stuff, you disciplined me; then you forgave my mistake in thinking these trivial studies to be fun. The fact is, I learned many useful words in these poems, but I might better have learned them in material that was not so vapid. For young boys, that is a safer route to follow.

17

Let me say something now, my God, about your gifts (my talents) and the nonsense on which they were being frittered away. I had been studying the classics gladly and willingly, and was considered a promising boy.* Then an assignment was handed to me that shook me up, for it promised me praise if I came out ahead, and disgrace and a beating if I didn't. I was to recite the words of Juno as she complained in sorrow and anger that she could not "turn back the threat to Italy by the Trojan king." I had already learned that Juno never spoke those words; yet we pupils were all compelled to stumble along in the footsteps of the poet and his fictions. We were expected to put into our own prose what the poet had rendered in verse. That boy was applauded who was able

* The phrase "a promising boy" comes from Section 16.

most dramatically to re-enact the passions of anger and grief, using language suitable to the character of the person involved.

Now, what is all that to me, my God, my true life? Why was my recitation acclaimed over those of many of my own age and class? Wasn't it all just so much wind and smoke? Couldn't they have found something better on which I could exercise my brain and tongue? Your praises, Lord, your praises through your Scriptures might have propped up the tender branches of my heart. They might have kept it from being snatched away by such asinine stuff, and so turned into the ugly prey of the vultures. There are more ways than one of sacrificing to the fallen angels!

18

It should be no great surprise, my God, that I was swept away from you into a useless kind of living. Men were held up as examples for me to imitate, who would appear covered with embarrassment if they used a crude expression or made a grammatical slip, though there would be nothing wrong with what they were discussing. But these same men would rattle on and on as they boasted about their sex life and would be warmly applauded for it, so long as they used correct and well-chosen words in their descriptions.

You see all these things, Lord, yet you say nothing, for you are slow to anger and full of mercy and truth.[31] Will you always remain silent? I know that answer. Even now you are pulling out of a bottomless hole someone who is searching for you and who is thirsting after your delights, and whose heart is saying to you, "When you said to me, 'Seek my face,' my heart said to you, 'Your face, Lord, do I seek.' "[32] At the time I was a long way from your face and my heart was dark. It is not our feet or a change in location that takes us away from you. That younger son in the parable [33] did not need horses or chariots or ships or wings; he did not even need to move his legs to get to the "far country" where he proposed to live it up and dissipate everything you had handed him at the start. You were a kind and loving Father when you gave, and even kinder and more loving when he returned to you penniless. But when the appetites are aroused and the heart is dark, it is a long way to your face.

Look, Lord my God, just look. Patiently. Look at the punctilious way the sons of men observe the literary code and all the syllable rules they've received from those who spoke the tongue before them. Then see how they neglect the eternal code of everlasting salvation they received from you. Anyone who teaches or studies the traditional pronunciation, but drops his "aitches" and says " 'uman being" instead of "human being" (thereby breaking a rule of grammar) [34] is considered more offensive than a person who hates his fellow man (thereby breaking a rule of yours). No enemy can destroy a man so thoroughly as the man's own hate-feelings that created the enemy in the first place. No man can damage the enemy he persecutes so severely as he damages his own soul by the buildup of his inner hostility. And there is certainly no literary attainment to match the inner handwriting of the conscience that tells a man to avoid doing to someone else what he would not wish done to himself.

How mysterious you are in your solitary majesty and your silence, God "that dwellest in the heavens." [35] By a relentless law you decree the loss of [spiritual] sight as a punishment for illicit desire. But a man, on the other hand, will stand before a very human judge, surrounded by a crowd, and spew out his venom against his enemy; and because he is aiming at a reputation for eloquence, he will be very careful not to make a slip of the tongue by murdering a word like "human being." Yet if the fury of his feeling succeeds in actually bringing about the murder of his enemy (a human being!) he will not give it a second thought.

19

Such were the manners of the world at whose threshold I lay, an unhappy boy; and such was the school in which I was being trained.

In those days I was a great deal more concerned to avoid a grammatical slip of the tongue than I was to avoid the sin of envying some other boy when I made a slip and he didn't. I say this and confess it to you, my God. I was petted and praised by the people whom I most wanted to impress, but failed to see the sinkhole into which I was sliding, far from your inspection. Could anything be more obnoxious in your sight than I was—I who failed to win acceptance even by my peers? I told any number of lies to my tutor, my masters, and my parents—all for the love of sport and stage spectacles, and from a restless itch to imitate those who took part in these stupid events. I stole from my parents' cellar and table, sometimes just because I was a glutton, sometimes because I wanted to have something to trade with other boys for playthings they were willing to sell, even though they loved them as much as I did. When I was being outplayed I tried to win games by cheating, because I had an insatiable desire to come out ahead. If I caught anyone else cheating, of course, I became furious and told him off in no uncertain terms. But when I was caught myself, I would start up an argument rather than admit I was wrong.

Is this the innocence of boyhood? It is not, Lord. It is not! Lord, have mercy. For as we grow to adulthood these are the kinds of offenses we continue to commit, no longer against tutors and teachers, no longer over nuts and balls and sparrows, but now against kings and governors in a struggle for gold and land and slaves. The whip our schoolmaster used is now replaced by more severe penalties. It seems when you, our King, once said, "Of such is the kingdom of heaven," you were approving the humility of a child,[36] symbolized by his small stature—but were hardly approving his "innocence"!

20

Even if it had not been your will that I should live beyond boyhood, I would still owe thanks to you, most excellent Lord our God, architect and ruler of the universe. For after all, I did exist, I did live, I did feel, and I was concerned about the welfare of my being. There were traces within me of that mysterious unity from which I originally came. Inward common sense kept watch, as it were, over the integrity of external sensory reactions. As I deliberated over and participated in little matters, I learned to take delight in the truth. I had an active memory, spoke with a good vocabulary, hated to be proved wrong, enjoyed my friends, and avoided bad news, ignorance, and plain meanness.

Is not such a creature admirable? Is he not worthy of praise? But all these were gifts from the hand of my God; I did not give them to myself. They were all good, and together they made up what was me. So I would say that the One who made me is good, and he is *my* good. I shall exult in joy over every worthwhile thing that can be attributed to me as a boy. But here was my sin: I sought for pleasure, honor, and truth, not in God but in his creatures, including myself and others, and so fell into sorrow, confusion, and error. So now I give thanks to you, my joy, my confidence, my God, thanks to you for your gifts—and will you please sustain them in me? For in this way you will keep me safe, and develop and mature that which you have given; and I shall be with you, who gave me life in the first place.

BOOK TWO

The Pears of Adolescence

1

I will now look back over what is past and done with, my messed-up life and all the sensual corruption that went on in my heart—not because I relish the prospect, but so that I might love you, my God. Analyzing such good-for-nothing behavior is a bitter undertaking, but it is done for love of your love, so that you might grow sweet and lovely to me. Yours is a loveliness that never lets me down, a loveliness wrapped in security and happiness. So once again you, the great Unifier, must show how you put together my fragmented personality after it turned away from you and split into pieces and became lost.

As I grew into adolescence I took my fill of hell. I ran wild in a rank forest of shady amorous adventures, and my beauty consumed away like a moth.[1] As I tried to create an attractive image in my own eyes and in the eyes of men, I turned into something rotten in your eyes.

2

What did I really want? Nothing except to love and be loved. But I failed to set up the heart-to-heart relationship that marks the bright trail of friendship. Instead, out of the slimy potholes of the flesh and the geysers of puberty there arose vapors that exhaled upon and covered over and obscured my heart, so that I could not tell the blue skies of real love from the polluted overcast of my appetites. Both were mixed up inside me in confusion, and together they lured my immature youth over the precipice of sexual desire and dropped me in a whirlpool of shame and disgrace. Without my knowing it, your anger had risen and was towering over me. I was deafened by the clanking chains of my mortality, which had become the punishment of my proud spirit. So I went farther away from you, and you just let me go. I was tossed back and forth, spilling, squandering, and wasting in my fornicating, and you held your peace. Why so late in coming, O my Joy? You continued to be silent while I, arrogant, dejected, restless, and sick of it all, kept straying farther and farther from you, and more and more into the sandy soil of a deep, inner anguish.

If only someone could have modulated my dismal condition, and turned what fleeting good there was in those experiences into useful channels, and fixed limits for their delights! Then the waves of my billowing youth might have rolled in on the shoreline of marriage. Then my sex drives might have been tranquilized and fulfilled by having a family, just as your law prescribes, Lord. (With what a tender hand you are able to blunt the thorns that were excluded from your Paradise! Even when we are a long way from you, your Omnipotence is never far away from us.)

Or, I might have paid more attention to the thunder of your Scriptures: "Those who marry shall have tribulation in the flesh." . . . "It is good for a man not to touch a woman." . . . "The unmarried cares for the things of the Lord, how he can please the Lord, but the married cares for the things of the world, how he can please his wife." [2] I might have paid more attention to these voices. I might even have unsexed myself for the Kingdom of God,[3] so I could look forward more happily to your loving embrace.

But fool that I was, I followed the impulses of my unstable nature, left you behind, and broke all your laws—though I did not escape your whip. What mortal does? You were always there, angry yet merciful, adding a bitter and offensive flavor to all my illicit pleasures, so that I might turn and seek those pleasures that would not give offense. But where could I find them except in you, Lord, except in you? You teach us our lessons by sorrow; you wound us to heal us; you kill us that we might not die apart from you.

Anyway, that is where I stood in the sixteenth year of my life, exiled from the delights of your house, and sold out to the wild sexuality that held sway over me. It was a wildness that indulged disgraceful conduct, though it received no indulgence from your laws. Meanwhile my people made no effort to rescue me by marriage; their sole concern was to have me learn how to become a persuasive orator who would make the best possible kind of speech.

3

In that year my studies were interrupted. I had come back home from Madaura, a neighboring city where I had been sent to study grammar and rhetoric. Now the expenses were being got together by my father to send me to Carthage, a farther distance away. My father's spirit outran his means in this project, as he was a mere humble freeman of Thagaste. To whom am I telling all this? Not to you, my God, but I tell it before you to my fellow men, to the human race—rather, to that small part of it that might chance to come across these writings of mine. And why do I tell it? Obviously so that I, and whoever reads, may gain some understanding of the profound depths from which we must lift our cry to you. What is more certain to be heard by you than a confessing heart in a life of faith? My father merits honor and credit for going considerably beyond the limit of his means to provide his son with the expenses for going away to school. Many a wealthier citizen failed to do as much for his children. Yet my father never took any interest in how

I was growing toward you, or what state my morals were in. So long as I grew in eloquence, it didn't seem to matter how barren I was to your cultivation, God; yet you are the one true and worthy Lord of your meadow which is my heart.

During that sixteenth year I was forced by my parents' financial straits to drop out of school and live at home with nothing to do. There the thorny branches of sex and temptation trapped me in a briar patch that grew over my head, and no hands were available to root them out. In fact, when my father saw me one day in the public baths, stripped, and discovered that I had reached the age of puberty and adolescence, his reaction was quite a happy one. He went home and told my mother about it, and began looking forward eagerly to grandchildren. Thus does the world forget you, its Creator, and falls in love with what you have created instead of with you. But in my mother's heart you had already started to build your temple and had laid the foundation of your holy habitation; while my father was but a beginning inquirer. Mother was, as a result, shaken up with holy fear and trembling. She knew I was not yet a believer, and she dreaded those twisted paths used by men who walk with their backs toward you and not their faces.

Oh, me! I don't suppose I dare claim that you had nothing to say, my God, while I kept wandering farther from you. Were you really silent? Whose words were they that my mother, your faithful one, kept sounding in my ears, if they weren't yours? Not that any of them ever reached my heart or had any effect on me. I remember her counseling me privately and expressing her deep concern that I should not indulge in fornication, and especially that I should never commit adultery with another man's wife. But it sounded to me like female talk and to conform to it would have made me blush.

Of course they were your words, but I didn't know it. I thought you were mute and she was doing the talking, but now I know you were not silent, but were speaking to me through her. So when her advice was rejected it meant you were being despised by me—by me, her son, the son of your handmaid, your servant.[4] But I didn't know, and went blindly on my headlong course. I was ashamed to be less scandalous than my friends, whom I heard bragging about their disgusting exploits; and the more disgusting the episodes were, the more they bragged about them. So I did the same things they did, not simply for the pleasure of doing them, but mostly for the praise I hoped to get. What deserves faultfinding more than finding fault? I made myself out to be worse than I was, so that I might be praised for it; and when I didn't actually stoop to their lowest level, I would pretend to have done what I didn't do. In that way I tried to avoid being a contemptible coward in my friends' eyes, when (for the moment) I was innocent and chaste. The companions with whom I tramped the streets of Babylon were certainly nothing to boast about. We reeled and wallowed about in the filth as though it were cinnamon * or expensive perfume. To make sure I would get stranded in the heart of the city, my invisible enemy trampled me and seduced me; and I was easy to seduce.

Meanwhile my mother had taken flight from the center of Babylon, though she continued to dally in the city's outskirts.[5] Even while she warned me to keep my virtue, she forgot what my father had told her about me. She was aware that my sexual drives were creating problems for me and were full of dangerous possibilities for the future, but she didn't think it wise at the time to put them on leash within the bounds of married love (assuming they could not be cut back to the quick).[6] My mother took no action because she was afraid that a wife would be a hindrance and stumbling block to my career—not to those hopes of a future life which she had in you, Lord, but to her hopes for me academically.

Both my parents were very much concerned about my studies— my father because he almost never thought about you and had shallow enough thoughts about me; my mother because she judged that

---

* Cinnamon was in Augustine's day (and still is) one of the most popular among the spices of the East. At one time it was considered more valuable than gold.

the normal course of my studies would be no personal detriment, but could very well help me to find you. To the best of my recollection, that's the way I interpret the inclination of my parents at the time. In any case I was free to do as I liked without proper restraints, and so fell into loose habits and got generally knocked about. And in all of this, my God, a heavy mist shut off my view of the brightness of your truth, while my sins ballooned out in fatness.[7]

4

Robbery is punishable by your law, Lord, and by the law written in the hearts of men which cannot be blotted out by evil, no matter how hard the effort. What's more, no thief can stand being robbed by another thief, even if the one happens to be rich and the other in desperate want. I chose to steal not because I was compelled to by poverty or hunger, but just from a bellyful of sin and a contempt for justice. I stole what I already had plenty of—and what I had was in better condition. I didn't take any pleasure in what I stole—just enjoyed the stealing and the sinning.

A pear tree grew near our orchard, loaded with fruit. One night some of us young mischief-makers, who were used to staying out on the streets and playing until very late, decided to knock down the pears on that tree and carry them off. We carted away a huge load, not to eat but to throw at the hogs. For our part we barely tasted them; our chief pleasure was derived from the knowledge that we had done what was forbidden.

Such was my heart, God, such was my heart on which you had mercy when it was down at the bottom of the deep. Let that heart now confess to you what it was after: It would engage in wrongdoing for no reason or provocation, and sin just for the fun of sinning. It was vile and I loved it. I loved my destruction. I loved my failure—not the act of failing, but the failure itself. I was a headstrong kid who left the security that was in you and plunged toward disaster, eager for nothing from my dishonorable conduct but the dishonor itself.

5

There is an attractiveness in beautiful things, in gold and silver and the rest. The sense of touch conveys its own powerful pleasure; the other senses find enjoyment in different material objects. Worldly success brings its glory with it, and so does the power to command and overcome; out of them springs the longing for a man's vindication. But in reaching for all these normal desires we ought not to depart from you, Lord, or deviate from your law. The appeal of the life we live here on earth is based on the extent of its natural beauty and the harmony it establishes with other elements of beauty. The bond of human friendship has an endearing quality, as it makes many hearts beat as one. But again, all these goals can lead to the committing of sin if, by overstressing them, we abandon life's higher and better qualities—and even abandon you, our Lord God, and your truth and your law. These lesser things may have splendid characteristics, but are not to be compared with my God, who made them all. "The righteous shall be glad in the Lord . . . and all the upright in heart shall glory." [8]

Now when we investigate the motive of a crime, we are not usually satisfied unless it can be proved that it was prompted by a desire to gain some of these "lesser things"—or by the fear of losing them. Beautiful and fascinating as such goals are, they are mean and contemptible when compared with the higher spiritual values. But here is a man who commits murder. Why did he do it? Because he wanted the other man's wife or his land; or because he felt he had to steal to live; or he was afraid of losing something to his victim; or perhaps he felt he had been wronged and burned for revenge.

Would a man commit murder without cause, just for the delight of murdering someone? Incredible! Even in the record of that savage and brutal man Catiline [9] a motive was provided. Catiline had a reputation for being cruel without any justification; yet he reportedly explained his behavior "lest through idleness his hand or heart should become apathetic." [10] And what was his end in view? To capture the city of Rome by his criminal deeds, and achieve honors, wealth, and empire; to escape the fear of the law; to avoid the financial difficulties that kept his family in want; and to wipe out the consciousness of his crimes. So even Catiline loved not his atrocities but something else that made him commit them.

6

What was it about the pear theft that appealed to unhappy fifteen-year-old me? Granted, the pears we stole were attractive, for they were created by you, the Creator of all, the most beautiful of all, the good God, the supremely good God, and my own true good. Yes, they were attractive, but it was hardly for pears that my forlorn soul pined—I already had better pears of my own. What I picked, I picked simply to steal and throw away. The only pleasure I took in eating them was the taste of my sin, for if any of those pears entered my mouth, it was the sin that sweetened them. But now, Lord my God, I would like to know what it was that gave me satisfaction in the robbery, since it had no attractiveness of its own. Let's not compare it with the very real beauty there is in justice and wisdom, in the mind and its memory, in the sensory and biological life of man, in the glorious majesty of the stars in their courses, or in the earth and sea, teeming with life that moves through its cycle of birth and death. To be quite honest, this little act of mine did not even have the enticing, shady, counterfeit kind of charm that vice so often uses to deceive us.

For human pride also deceives us with the mask of a lofty

spirit, not realizing that you, God, are the only loftiness there is. In the same way human ambition seeks honor and glory, not knowing that you are to be honored above all things and glorified forever. The great ones aim to create fear by cruelty, yet who is to be feared but God alone? What can be snatched away and stolen from his power? When? Where? How? By whom? The caresses of the sporting-house inhabitants * are an attempt at love; but what can compare with the caresses of your love? Nor is there anything healthier than the love of your bright and beautiful truth.

Curiosity appears to prompt a desire for scientific knowledge, whereas you are all knowledge in yourself, supremely. Under the guise of "simplicity" and "innocence" are often found stupidity and ignorance; but where is a simplicity like yours? Who is more innocent and blameless than you, since it is the sinner's own sins that injure him? Laziness pretends to a craving for rest; but what sure rest is there outside the Lord? Luxury would like to be branded as abundance and satisfaction, but you are the inexhaustible supply of the abundance of unfading delights. Extravagance makes a play at being generous, but you are the free-spending, affluent giver of all good. Avarice wants to grab everything, but you already have it all. Envy tries for excellence, but what is so excellent as you? Anger seeks revenge, but whose vengeance is so just as yours? Fear shudders at the strange and unexpected, which poses a threat to something beloved and causes security precautions to be taken; but what can take you by surprise? What can separate you from that which you love? Where is there security except with you? Sadness, grieving over the loss of things that please desire, is unwilling to give up anything; but from you nothing can ever be taken away.

Thus the soul goes whoring when it turns away from you. It looks somewhere else for that which can never be found in pure

* The original meaning of the Latin verb *lascivio* was "to play" or "to sport"; but as Augustine used the noun *lascivientius*, it meant a lustful or wanton person such as a prostitute. I have sought to bring out the two senses in translation.

and pristine form until the soul comes back again to you. Even those who turn their backs on you and exalt themselves against you are, in a perverted way, copying you. They can't help declaring by their very imitating that you are the Creator of the universe, and there is nowhere they can go to get away from you. So I come back to the question: What was it that attracted me to that pear robbery? In what twisted and defective way was I trying to imitate my Lord? Did I think it would be fun to try to break your law, even though I was powerless to do so? Perhaps that was it: I wanted the kind of pleasure a prisoner might gain by dreaming he was a free man, and that he had violated the law without being punished. That would give him a false sense of omnipotence—but what a horrible way to live! What a yawning death trap! Why did I have to like what was forbidden just because it was forbidden?

7

What shall I render unto the Lord [11] for making it possible to recollect these memories, while my soul remains completely free from fear? I shall love you, Lord, and give thanks to you and confess your name, because you have forgiven me the many evil things I have done. Your Grace and your memory are responsible for melting the ice of my sins. Your Grace even accounts for the fact that there was some evil that I did not do—for who knows what I might have done, seeing that I loved sin for its own sake?

And now I declare that everything has been forgiven me, both the evil I did on purpose, and the evil I might have done if you hadn't stopped me. Considering the fickleness of human nature, what man would dare attribute his chaste and innocent behavior to his own manly powers? It would not only make him love you less, it would make him appear less in need of your mercy than those who find their sins forgiven and are converted to you. So if any man has heard your voice and followed you, and avoided the things I have here confessed and recorded as having done, let him not deride me! I was sick, but I have been healed by the same Physician who kept such a man from being sick—or rather, less sick than I. For this reason let the man love you just as much and even more, since he sees that I've now been delivered from sin and weakness by the same Redeemer who kept him from it in the first place.

8

What fruit, then, did I have in the things of which I am now ashamed? [12] I am thinking particularly of that theft which in itself was nothing, but which made me all the more miserable because I loved being part of it. As I think back on how I felt then, I'm certain I never would have attempted it alone. I loved it because of the companionship of the fellows with whom I did it. In a sense, therefore, I did not love just the act of stealing itself; yet in another sense it was only the stealing I loved, for what did the companionship amount to? Nothing. Then what is the truth here? Who is it that can teach me, if not he who illuminates my heart and exposes every dark corner of it? What am I getting at in all this discussion? Let's go over it again: If I had loved the pears I made off with, and wanted to enjoy them, I might have stolen them all by myself. I would not have needed to rub the wits of my pals to start my own desires itching, if just stripping a tree would have served my fun. Obviously the fun did not come from the pears, so it must have come from the theft itself, as carried out in company with fellow sinners.

9

What exactly was this feeling of pleasure? It was corrupt, that is certain, and the rough part is, I had it. But what was it? "Who can understand his errors?" [13] We laughed because our minds were tickled at the joke we were playing on those who had no idea what we were doing, and who would have violently objected to it. But what fun was there in it, that I would not have found pulling it off by myself? Is it because nobody laughs easily when alone? That's not true; there are times when men can be completely by themselves, and be overcome with laughter at something ridiculous that appeals to the sense or mind. But alone I would not have done it, I would not have done it at all. Look, my God, at the record of my very heart open before you. I would not have committed the theft alone. My pleasure was not in *what* I stole, but *that* I stole. Alone it wouldn't have been any fun at all, and I never would have got into it.

O friendship most unfriendly, that seduces the mind in a way we don't understand, that can't wait to get us into trouble just for "the hell of it," that wants to cause loss to someone else without any motive of getting even or personal gain! Somebody says, "Come on, let's do it!" and we are ashamed not to be shameless.

10

Who can untangle such a twisted snarl of knots? It is so fouled up I hate to look at it or think about it. I want you, Justice and Purity, who are beauty and loveliness to eyes that can truly see. I want you with a satisfaction not quite satisfied in this life. In you there is real rest, in you there is life and peace. Whoever enters into you enters into the joy of his Lord [14] and has no need to fear; he shall achieve his best in the Lord who is the best.

My God, I deserted you in my youth. I wandered too far from your steadfast help, and became to myself a blighted land.

BOOK THREE

The Young Carthaginian

1

I came to Carthage * and found a seething vat of sexual immorality bubbling all around me. I was not yet in love, but was in love with love, and naturally in such a state was looking for someone to love. Security I despised; what did I want with a life free from traps and pitfalls? Within me there was a deep hunger caused by a lack of that spiritual food which is yourself, my God—yet I was not aware of it. I felt no desire whatever for the Living Bread, not because I had plenty, but because the more I went without it, the more I seemed to loathe it. My soul was in weak and puny shape, its ulcers dripping, as it itched for some sensual contact on which it could scrape itself.

Yet even in this kind of condition my soul sought to satisfy its hunger for love. To love and be loved became my chief delight in life, especially when I was able to enjoy the body of the one who loved me. So I polluted the stream of friendship with the sludge of unbridled sex, and tarnished its brilliance with my infernal lust. No matter how badly I behaved, I still was vain enough to keep posing as a refined and courtly type. Then what I had longed for

* Carthage, to which Augustine came in A.D. 370 as a sixteen-year-old student, was one of the flourishing cities of the Roman Empire, with many churches and a population of several hundred thousand. In North Africa only Alexandria could challenge Carthage's role. The city was finally destroyed by the Arabs in A.D. 697.

happened: I fell head over heels in love. My God, my Compassion, how much bitterness you in your goodness managed to sprinkle on that sweet experience! For I was truly beloved, and our bond of love had reached a secret climax of delight. Yet those chains of joy also brought calamity to me, so that I was beaten with the rods of hot iron forged by jealousy, suspicion, fear, anger, and quarreling.

2

The dramatic spectacles in the amphitheater enthralled me by acting out my miseries and igniting my fires. Why is it that a man likes to be made sad by doleful and tragic sights that he cannot himself endure? As a spectator he wants to feel a sense of grief, and it is the grief that gives him pleasure. This is not just pitiful— it is crazy! The more the play affects him, the less he is able to preserve his emotional balance.

When a man suffers they call it misery; when he shares the suffering of someone else they call it compassion. What do they call it when he sees suffering feigned on the stage? Is this "compassion"? The spectator is not moved to help the sufferer, but merely to feel sorry for him; and the more the author makes the audience grieve, the better they like him. If the disasters that befall the characters (whether drawn from ancient history or out of the imagination) are depicted so poorly as not to touch the spectator and move him to tears, the patron goes away critical and disgusted; but if he is saddened, he stays to the end and is happy about the whole thing.

Is compassion then to be repudiated? By no means! The sorrows of others draw upon our love. But let my soul beware of uncleanness and stay under the shelter of my God, the God of our fathers, praise and exalt his name over all forever! I have not lost my compassion, but when I used to go to the theater I was happy for the lovers when they sinfully enjoyed each other, though it was all fictitious; and I wept for them when they lost each other; and either way I enjoyed it. Today I feel more pity for the man who delights in his sin than I do for the man who complains he isn't getting out of life what he wants, especially since the sensual pleasure most men seek is ultimately a waste and a misery. To feel such pity is true compassion, but it's nothing to enjoy. The person who has compassion for an unhappy individual deserves credit for his love, but a really compassionate person would wish that there were nothing to begin with to cause unhappiness. Grief, then, may be justified, but never loved. That is why you, Lord God, can love our souls with a purity we ourselves cannot match, because your mercy is unstained, and sorrow cannot injure you. But "who is sufficient for these things?" [1]

During those days, being depressed, I loved to indulge my mood and went out of my way to look for something to be sad about. Another man's misery (even though I knew it was phony and staged) was pleasant for me to watch; and the better the acting and the more vehement the performance, the more I would sit there and bawl. Was it any wonder that an unhappy sheep, straying from your fold, impatient at your oversight, should become infected with a scabby disease? [2] I loved being miserable, but didn't want the sorrow to cut too deep, because I couldn't stand to face my own problems. I just wanted to scratch the surface of my emotions lightly by hearing the humbug on the stage. Unfortunately the scratching, as if by dirty fingernails, produced an angry swelling and a poisonous infection. Such was my life—but was it life, my God?

3

While your faithful mercy overshadowed me from above, I ran myself ragged in misguided activities, following an irreverent curiosity that deserted you and was bent on dragging me down to the depths of unbelief. I sacrificed to demons and not to God, [3] but while I remained in their crooked service you kept pommeling

me. One day, just at the time your solemn rites were being celebrated, I dared to carry out within the walls of your church a lusty
piece of business that deserved death as its fruit.[4] You punished me
well for it, but not as well as I should have been disciplined, O my
exceeding Mercy, my God, my Refuge from the terrible dangers
among which I wandered with an arrogant stiff neck. So I got
still farther away from you, loving my ways and not yours, indulg-
ing in the "freedom" of a runaway slave.

The reputable course of studies in which I engaged was intended
to prepare me for a distinctive career in civil law. The idea was,
the more crooked I became, the greater would be my distinction.
I soon stood at the head of the school of rhetoric, a fact from
which I gained great pleasure and immense arrogance. Still I was
a lot more sedate than some—Lord, you know it—and quite separate from the destructive activities of such student groups as the
"Overturners"—that being the unpromising and diabolical name
which one group assumed as the ultimate badge of sophistication.
I actually lived among them with a kind of shameless shame because I didn't get involved in the things they did. I very much
enjoyed their friendship at times, but had little use for their
activities. One of their favorite tricks was to persecute the shy
incoming freshmen, and to mistreat them without any reason
whatever except to feed their own warped ideas of humor. Oh,
they were a devilish crew. "Overturners" was the right name for
them, since their life-style had been tipped upside down and perverted. As they amused themselves by mocking others and giving
them a bad time, they were being mocked by the same demonic
spirits they sought to serve.

4

In this unsettled kind of climate I studied the literature of eloquence, since I wanted to excel in that field for very human and
very ignoble reasons of pride. In the regular progress of my studies

I came across a book by a certain Cicero, whose language nearly everyone admires—but not his heart. The book contains an exhortation to philosophy and is titled *Hortensius*.[5] It affected me deeply and changed the whole character of the prayers I offered to you, giving me a fresh aim and purpose in life. Suddenly all my vain ambitions seemed worthless, and with a passionately burning heart I now craved immortal wisdom. I had begun the long upward journey that was to bring me back to you.

By this time I was eighteen years old. My father had been dead for two years, and I was receiving an allowance from my mother to continue my studies of rhetoric. It was not to sharpen the eloquence of my tongue that I read the *Hortensius*, however; what impressed me was the subject matter of the book rather than its style. How I burned inside, my God, how I burned to leave this earth by spreading my wings and soaring back to you—but I had no inkling of what you would be doing with me. "With him is wisdom and strength." [6]

The word "philosophy" means "love of wisdom," which is what the *Hortensius* kindled in me. There are pseudo-philosophers who claim that great and honorable title as a front to add prestige or color to their writings and to lead men astray. Almost all the word merchants of that sort in Cicero's day and earlier are named in his volume and exposed for what they are. In his work can also be discerned that healthy warning of your Spirit, spoken by your good and devout servant [Paul]: "See to it that no one makes a prey of you by philosophy and empty deceit, according to human tradition, according to the elements of the universe, and not according to Christ. For in him the whole fulness of deity dwells bodily." [7]

At that time as you know, Light of my heart, the writings of the Apostle were still unknown to me. So I delighted in the exhortation of Cicero which told me I should not go traipsing after this sect or that, but I should go for wisdom itself; that I should love it, seek it, get it, clasp it, and hold it, wherever it might be. The book excited me and warmed my heart. Only one thing checked the ardor of my enthusiasm: the name of Christ was not in it.

For in your mercy, Lord, the name of your Son, my Savior, had been taken into my tender heart as an infant along with my mother's milk, and retained. Whatever omitted that name, no matter how literary a piece it seemed to be or how polished or truthful, never really captured me.

5

I decided to apply myself to the study of Holy Scripture to see what it was like. What I discovered was not something to be grasped by the proud or the immature, but something veiled in mysteries, humbling as one enters and sublime as one advances. I was not one of those able to enter by bending my neck to negotiate the steps. For when I directed my attention to the Scripture I did not feel as I do now; it did not appear to me worthy of being compared to the dignity of Marcus Tullius Cicero. My sophisticated pride shrank from its literary style, and my trained wit was unable to penetrate its inner meaning. The Scripture is designed to help spiritual little ones to grow, but I couldn't stand the thought of being a "little one." Puffed up in arrogance as I was, I looked upon myself as one of the greats.

6

In Carthage I joined a group of inflated crackpots [the Manicheans *] whose chief characteristics were a loose lip and looser habits. These men made their mouths into snares of the devil, setting their traps by mixing the syllables of your name and the names of the Lord Jesus Christ and the Paraclete, the Holy Spirit. These names were always being bandied in their throats, but only

* Manicheism was at one time a formidable rival to Christianity. It was a philosophy of the universe expressed in terms of mythology, and appealed to imagination rather than to reason. Its founder was Mani (215-277), said to have been born in Babylonia of Iranian descent. While officially banned by Roman edict, the sect had become popular in North Africa in Augustine's day.

as guttural sounds and tongue noises. Their hearts were empty of truth. They prattled about "truth and truth!" and were forever repeating the word to me, but the truth was not in them.[8] They spoke lies not only about you, who really are the Truth, but also about the elements of the world, your creation.

O Truth, Truth, how deeply even then did I sigh and yearn after you in my innermost being. In so many different ways, and in so many vast tomes, these men sounded out your name to me, but it was all so much wind. While I got hungrier and hungrier for you, they served up instead of you, platters containing the sun and moon, your beautiful creations—but only your creations and not yourself.[9] Fantasies were what they served me on those platters. I might better have loved the sun, which is at least real to our sight, than their false illusions. The fantasies of the Manicheans were not at all like you, my God, as you have spoken to me now. They were material fantasies and false bodies; and it was on such empty stuff I was feeding without being fed.

Where were you then? How far away from me? I wandered so far from your presence that I was not even able to eat the husks that I fed the swine.[10] How much better than such soul-traps were the fables of the poets and the grammarians! For verses and songs I could turn into food for the mind even though I didn't believe them; but the pity of it is, I did believe the Manichean fantasies. I now confess it to you, my God, because you had mercy on me when I didn't confess it: I sought after you with my senses, but not with the understanding of the mind by which you have set us above the beasts. You were deeper inside me than the most intimate part of me, and higher than my highest reach.

7

Because I didn't know the meaning of spiritual reality, I was influenced in a subtle way to accept the views of these deceivers.

They would ask me such questions as, "Where does evil come from?" and, "Is God limited to a bodily shape,[11] and if so, does he have hair and nails?" and, "Do you call those Old Testament patriarchs just and upright men when they engaged in polygamy and slaughtered people and sacrificed animals?" In my ignorance I was bothered by these questions, imagining I was going toward the truth when actually I was backing away from it. I had not yet learned that evil is the absence of good. How could I learn it, when all I could see was material forms with the eye and imaginary forms with the mind? I had not discovered that God is Spirit, having no parts; for every mass is less in its part than in its whole, and so cannot be wholly itself in every place, as God is. I was completely ignorant of the scriptural teaching that the spirit of man within us is formed in the image of God.

Neither was I acquainted with that valid inner sense of justice that does not judge by usage or by habit, but by the excellent law of Almighty God. According to that law the customs of countries and epochs are shaped to meet their environmental needs, though the law itself is uniformly the same in time and space, and is not one thing in one place and another elsewhere. According to the same standard, Abraham and Isaac and Jacob and Moses and David and all those men whom God singled out for praise were just men, even though they are considered unjust by men who render a verdict from their own limited experience, and who gauge their judgment of universal human behavior from the partial standpoint of their own customs.

Such critics are like a man who outfits himself in an armory without knowing which piece of equipment goes on which part of the body, so he puts a shinguard on his head and a helmet on his shin, and then complains that they don't fit. Or they are like a shopkeeper who, when a legal holiday has been declared for the afternoon, becomes irritated because he can't sell his goods as he did in the morning. Or again, they are like a house-servant picking up something that another servant such as the winebearer is not allowed to touch.[12] Or they are like a man who does something behind a barn that is not allowed in the dining room. The point is that they are angry because in one house and in one family, the same things are not allowed to every member of the household or in all parts of the house. In exactly the same way, people are offended when they hear that something was permitted to just men in former times that is not permitted today. God gave one command to this man, and another to that man, as the times required; yet they both served the same cause of justice.

People should realize that in one household, in one day, different things are suitable for different members. An act might be lawful now, but not lawful an hour from now; or it might be permitted and commanded in this corner, but forbidden and punished in that corner. Does that mean justice is variable and changeable? No; it means that the times differ over which justice presides. But men, whose span on earth is brief, cannot by their own sense-impressions compare the conditions of past ages or of other nations —concerning which they have no expert knowledge—with the conditions they know. In the case of one body, or day, or family, they can see easily enough what differences would be necessary for each part of the body, or moment, or household, or person as the case might be. They will put up with such differences, and yet (inconsistently) take exception to the differences permitted by God's law as recorded in his Word.

These things I did not perceive or understand at the time. Though they battered my senses on every side, I failed to note them. I did not have the insight to discern that justice, which is served by all good and holy men, contains in itself the principle of all it prescribes without any variation. Yet that same justice does not prescribe everything at once, but allots to each age what is appropriate to each. Thus in my blindness I blamed those devout patriarchs of the Bible, not only for what they did during their lifetimes under the inspiration of God, but also for foretelling the future as God revealed it to them.

8

It is invariably right for a man to love God with his whole heart and mind and soul, and to love his neighbor as himself no matter where he is or what the circumstances. By the same token it is invariably wrong for a man to commit an offense contrary to nature and he should be punished for his detestable act no matter where he did it or when. Such was the crime of the Sodomites; and when other nations indulge in such behavior, they will be judged equally guilty of breaking God's law, for God did not make men in order that they might abuse each other. The friendship that ought to exist between God and man is violated when the nature God authored is polluted by lust and perversion. On the other hand, corrupt acts which violate the customs of men ought to be avoided according to the laws regulating those various customs.[13] If some rule of life is agreed to by custom or fixed by law in a city or nation, that rule should not be broken at the pleasure of a citizen or an alien. For each part offends that does not harmonize with the whole.

It is lawful for a reigning monarch to command something in his state which neither he nor anyone before him had ever commanded, and it is not considered contrary to the public interest to obey him. In fact, to disobey him would be to oppose the principles of human society, since obedience to princes is a general compact of such a society. That being the case, consider God, the ruler of the universe: How much more important it is to give unhesitating obedience to his commands! For if in the human chain of command the higher authority outranks the lower, then God, who outranks us all, is entitled to the obedience of us all.

In criminal acts there is intent to injure someone else, whether by insult or by violence. In either case the crime is committed for the sake of getting even (as one enemy attacking another), or gaining advantage (as a highway bandit over a traveler), or from fear (as one who would avoid danger), or from envy (as when an underprivileged person attacks someone prosperous and well off, or when a wealthy man attacks a rival who threatens to become his equal), or simply for the sake of enjoying another person's suffering (as the spectators do at the gladiatorial games, or others do who ridicule and laugh at people). These are the main shoots of evil which sprout from the lust of the flesh, the lust of the eyes, and the pride of life,[14] or from any one or a combination of them. By these we sin against the "psaltery of ten strings," your Ten Commandments, God most high and most gracious.

But what acts of personal degradation can offend you, who are beyond corruption? And what crimes can injure you, who are beyond their reach? When men sin against themselves and damage their personalities, they draw down your retribution, with the result that their sin plays itself false; it injures only itself. Such men corrupt and pervert their own nature which you created and established. They either make improper use of things allowable, or develop a ravening appetite for things not permitted and contrary to nature. When found guilty, these men blow their tops mentally and verbally and kick against the spurs;[15] or they may throw off all the restraints of human society and go their high-handed way, creating private agreements or feuds according to their own likes or dislikes.

Such are the consequences when we depart from you, the fountain of life, the one true Creator and Sovereign of the universe. Such is the result when, through selfish pride, a part is falsely assumed to be the whole only because it is loved. We must return to you in humble devotion, and let you clean up our wrong habits. You, being full of compassion, forgive our iniquity.[16] You hear the groaning of the prisoners and loose us from the fetters we have made for ourselves.[17] This you do unless we raise against you the trumpet of a false liberty; and unless in our greed and lust to have more, we risk the loss of what we have because we prefer our own private good to you, who are everyone's good.

9

With these loathsome acts that corrupt the personality and the crimes against other people may be lumped many other iniquities. But there are also the faulty activities of youth, which discriminating adults will both censure from the standpoint of maturity and commend for their promise of better things, likening them to green blades of young wheat. And there are other acts that resemble sins against nature or our fellow man but are not strictly sins, for they offend neither you, our Lord God, nor social custom.

For example, when men set out to procure supplies for their ordinary living needs, we cannot simply accuse them of a craving to own things. Again, when the constituted authority punishes certain kinds of behavior, we cannot say with certainty that there was also a desire to inflict injury. Thus many actions which appear to men to be wrong are given the testimony of your approval, Lord; and many actions that are praised by men are damned by you, as you know. The appearance of the act may be different from what the perpetrator intended, and our knowledge of the special circumstances surrounding it may be lacking. But when you suddenly issue a command about something unusual and unforeseen, even though you may have forbidden it earlier, who doubts that it ought to be carried out? [18] You may conceal the reason for your order, and it may seem to violate the code of justice of human society, but a society is truly just only as it obeys you.

Happy are those who know for certain that you have commanded them! As for the men of the Bible, what they did was intended to reveal truths needed in their day, or to prophesy of things to come in the future.

10

Of all this I knew nothing, and so I mocked those holy servants and prophets of yours. But what did I gain by mocking them, except to be mocked by you, as little by little I was led without realizing it into [the Manicheans'] nonsense? I was stupid enough to believe that greater mercy was shown by you to the fruits of the earth than to men, for whom the fruits were created. And if a hungry man begged me for food, if he were not a Manichean, I would consider any food that I gave him accursed.

11

Then you "stretched forth your hand from above" [19] and drew up my soul from the dark abyss.[20] That faithful servant of yours, my mother, came to you in my behalf with more tears than most mothers shed at a child's funeral. Her faith in you had made plain to her that I was spiritually dead. And you heard her, Lord, you heard her. You didn't ignore the tears that fell from her eyes and watered the earth everywhere she prayed. You heard her and sent her a dream that so relieved her mind that she allowed me to live with her and to eat at the same table in the house. That was something she had refused to permit for some time because she so loathed the blasphemy and error in which I was swimming.

In her dream she saw herself standing on a kind of measuring rule or wooden yardstick,[21] wailing and overcome with grief. A radiant young man approached her in a happy and laughing mood and asked her the reason for all this protracted weeping. (His purpose was not to learn from her but to teach her, as is customary in such dreams.) She replied that she was mourning the ruin of my soul. He then admonished her and, in a reassuring way, ordered her to look more carefully and she would see that I was standing precisely where she was. When she did look, she saw me standing next to her on the same measuring rule. Where did this dream come from, if you, Lord, did not "cause your ear to hear" and so prepare her heart? [22] O you Omnipotent Goodness, you care for us all as if each of us were your only concern, and you look after each of us as if we were all one person!

When Mother told me about her dream, I tried to disparage it, saying I interpreted it to mean she shouldn't give up hope, because one day she would be as I was [a Manichean]. She, however, came back at me immediately, saying, "No, it was not told me, 'Where he is, there you will be,' but rather, 'Where you are, there he will be.'" And this too I take to have come from you. I confess to you, Lord, that to the best of my memory (and I have often spoken of it) your answer which you gave through my mother impressed me more than the dream itself. She was not disturbed by my misinterpretation, because she had quickly grasped the meaning of the dream, which I had not seen until she spoke. So the joy that was to come to that godly woman years later was predicted as a consolation for the anguish I was causing her at the time.

Nearly nine years were to pass during which I sank deeper into the mire [23] and false darkness. I tried to climb out, but each time I fell backward and sprawled in the muck. And all the while this devout, gentle, modest widow (and such you love) was heartened by this hope. She never stopped her sighing and weeping; she never stopped beseeching you at all hours of the day and night, pounding away on my behalf before your presence. I know her prayers came before you,[24] and yet you still abandoned me to the pitch and roll of the darkness.

12

I remember one other answer to prayer that you gave my mother. You gave it to her through your holy servant, a certain bishop who had been brought up in the church and was well trained in your Scriptures.[25] This woman, my mother, went to him and asked if he would please have a talk with me. She wanted him to refute my errors, to show me where I was mixed up in my thinking, and so set me straight. It seems he often did this when he found the kind of people who were open to receive his instruction.

However, the bishop refused to see me—very wisely, as I later came to believe. He told her that at that time I was unteachable because I was all puffed up with the novelty of my weird ideas, and that I had already harassed and upset a number of immature persons with my questions, as she had indicated to him. "But," he said, "let him alone. Just keep praying to the Lord for him. He will discover through his reading what his error is, and how God looks at it." At the same time he went on to tell her that his own mother had been a Christian but she had been subverted by the Manicheans while he was still young. Not only had he read practically all the Manicheans' books, he had actually copied them out. Then he had come to the realization, without debate or argument with anyone else, that he would have to leave the sect; so he left it. After he said this to my mother, she was still not satisfied; she kept crying and pleading all the more, asking him to see me and talk with me. Finally he became weary and irritated with her and said, "Now go. As sure as you are alive, it is not possible that the son of these tears should be lost." As she often told me afterward, she accepted the answer as if it were a voice from heaven.

BOOK FOUR

The Rhetor as Dilettante

1

During that nine-year period from my nineteenth year to my twenty-eighth, I got completely off course and managed to lead some others astray as well. "Deceiving and being deceived," [1] I involved myself in various ambitious projects, some publicly through the teaching of what are called liberal arts, [2] some secretly under the false name of religion. In the one I was proud of myself, in the other superstitious, and in all things vain. Publicly I went after the empty shell of popular glory and the applause of the theater. I entered poetic contests. I competed for quickly fading crowns, for the spectacular frippery of the stage, and for the unbridled objectives of sex. Privately I sought to be purged of these shabby pursuits by carrying food to those [Manicheans] who were called "elect" and "saints." In their paunchy intestinal laboratories, these holy individuals were supposed to digest that food into angels and gods that would set us free.

My own friends and I cultivated this kind of behavior, they being deceived both through me and with me. Let the arrogant laugh at me, together with those who were never brought low and broken by you, my God, that they might be saved. I will confess my shame to you and glory in your praise. [3] I ask only that you stay with me, and give me now the ability to retrace in memory the circuitous route of my past errors and to offer you the "sacrifice of thanksgiving." [4] What am I without you, but a guide to my own ruination? What am I even at best, but a child suckling on your milk and feeding on you, the Food that never perishes? And what kind of man is he who is only a man and nothing more? Let the strong and mighty go ahead and laugh; but let us who are poor and needy [5] confess our need of you.

2

In those years I taught the art of rhetoric. Mastered by a desire for money, I put on the market a skill in speech that would master others. Yet you know, Lord, that I really preferred good students, if I may use that term; and that without tricks I taught the trickery of speechmaking—not to be used against the life of an innocent man, but sometimes to save the life of the guilty. And you, God, saw me from far off, stumbling on that slippery path, and sending up a tiny spark of faith amid a great billowing of smoke. I showed that spark by the diligent way I taught men who loved vanity and told lies [6]—I being one of them.

In those years I also had a mistress. She was not one to whom I was legally joined in marriage, but just someone my roving ardor and indifferent judgment picked up. Even so she was the only one, and I remained faithful to her. I found out by experience what a difference there is between the marriage covenant, entered into for the sake of the children, and a free love arrangement. When children are born to such an arrangement they come unwanted into the world—although once they are born, they compel us to love them.

There came a time when I decided to enter a poetry competition that involved reciting from the stage, and some fortune-teller (I have forgotten his name) sent me a message asking how much I would reimburse him to guarantee my winning the prize. It seems he would have killed certain animals, and by offering them as sacrifices, would have invited the demons to support me. I despised and scorned the practice of such disgusting hocus-pocus, and told him, "Even if the victor's crown were pure gold that would last forever, I wouldn't permit a fly to be put to death to help me win it."

God of my heart, it was no act of purity toward you on my part that caused me to reject this evil proposition. I didn't know how to love you, because I didn't know how to conceive the existence of anything—however glorious—beyond mere matter. The soul that goes puffing and wheezing after such figments of the imagination [as fortune-telling] is one that goes whoring from you,[7] and trusts what is phony, and feeds on the wind.[8] Yet while I wouldn't have this sorcerer sacrificing to demons on my behalf, I was actually sacrificing to them myself just by being involved in my superstition. For what else is it to feed on the wind, if not to feed on error, and so to become the sport and plaything of the demonic?

3

I did not hesitate, however, to consult those charlatans who are called astrologers,[9] because they made no sacrifices and offered no prayers to any spirit in their divining acts. Even so a genuine Christian faith rejects and damns their practice on principle. It is good to confess to you, Lord, and say, "Have mercy on me, heal my soul, for I have sinned against you." [10] It is good not to abuse the divine indulgence as a license to sin, but to remember the Lord's saying, "Behold, you are made whole; sin no more, lest some worse thing happen to you." [11] But all this healthful teaching the astrologers try to undermine by saying, "The stars inevitably cause you to sin," and, "Venus did this," or, "Saturn did this," or, "Mars did this." Obviously man, despite his flesh and blood and rotting pride, is without fault, because the fault lies with the Creator and Sustainer of the starry heavens! And who is he but our God, the source of justice and delight, who renders to every man according to his works and does not despise the broken and the contrite heart? [12]

At that time there lived in Carthage a wise man whose skill in the medical arts had won him fame in the region.[13] As the Roman proconsul he had placed on my unsound head the victor's wreath I had won in the poetry contest. He was not my physician, for you alone can cure men of my kind of sickness: you who resist the proud and give Grace to the humble.[14] Yet you did not let me down even through that old man, or neglect to use him to heal my soul. As I became better acquainted with him I began to listen to his words eagerly, for while his speech was simple, it was cultivated; while grave, it was also gay; and the very vivacity of his thought kept me enthralled. From our conversation he learned that I was given over to reading the astrologers, and in the kindest, most fatherly manner he advised me to throw their books away. He suggested that I should not waste time and effort on such trash that might better be spent on more useful things.

He told me that in his younger days he had studied the astrologers' arts and had considered entering the field professionally. Since he had absorbed the teachings of Hippocrates, he was quite able to understand the literature of astrology. Later he abandoned his idea and followed the practice of medicine, for the reason that he found astrology to be false to the core, and as a man of serious integrity he had no desire to earn his living by defrauding other men. "But you," he said, "can support yourself by your rhetoric, so you are dabbling in this asinine stuff of your own free will. That is all the more reason why you ought to believe me, for I intended to make my living at it, and went into the subject in depth to master the material." When I asked him why it was that astrology was able to predict many things with accuracy, he answered, sensibly enough, that the force of chance was diffused throughout the whole natural order. Sometimes, he said, a man would open the pages of a poet at random, and find a verse that seemed remarkably timely and con-

genial to the business at hand, although the poet himself was singing and reflecting about something quite different. It would not be
any more surprising, he concluded, if out of the mind of man some
powerful instinct from the unconscious would turn up an answer,
not by design but by chance, that would suit the business and actions of a seeker.[15] And thus either from him or through him, you
managed this matter for me and sketched in outline in my memory
what I later found out for myself. At the time neither he nor my
close friend Nebridius, an outstanding young man of high character
who laughed at the whole apparatus of divination, could persuade
me to drop it. The authority of the astrological writers impressed
me more than my friends did. I still had not come upon any docu-
mented proof, such as I sought, to satisfy me that beyond doubt
the happenings the astrologers accurately predicted were mere
chance or coincidence, and had nothing to do with the art of star-
gazing.

4

In those years I started teaching grammar in the city of my birth,
Thagaste. There I became attached to another close friend who,
like myself, had arrived at the flower of young manhood; and with
whom I shared both studies and outside interests. Actually we had
grown up together as boys, had gone to school and played together.
In childhood, however, he was not such an intimate friend as he
later became, though even our later relationship could hardly be
described in the truest sense as friendship. That, my God, is because true friendship exists only when you solder it together, and
when human hearts stick to you in the love that has been "poured
into our hearts through the Holy Spirit which has been given to
us." [16]

Still it was a very dear friendship to us, ripened by the warmth of
our common interests. I managed to deflect him from the Christian

faith, which he had not really accepted internally; and so got him tangled in the superstitions and destructive fables that had kept my mother in tears over me. His mind wandered into error together with mine, until my soul could not get along without him. But all the while you were close behind your fugitives, for you are a God of vengeance and a Fountain of mercy. You convert us to yourself in wonderful ways. Thus when our friendship had scarcely completed its first year you took him away, out of this life, and cut off what I valued as sweet above everything else in existence.

Who is there that can, through his own personal experiences, really "show forth all your praise"? [17] What did you do at that time, my God? "How unsearchable are your judgments, and your ways past finding out." [18] For my friend was stricken with a fever and for a long time lay unconscious in a lethal sweat. Then one day when his life was despaired of, without his being aware of it, he was baptized. I paid no attention to the incident, for I assumed that he would naturally retain what he had imbibed from me, and would hardly be affected by something performed on his body while he lay senseless. But things turned out differently. He began to recover his health and immediately, as soon as I was able to speak with him (which I could do because I never left him; in fact we hung onto each other too much for our own good), I tried to joke with him. I thought he would be ready to laugh with me at the baptism which (as he had learned) he had received while lying there incapable of thought or feeling. But he drew away from me horrified as if I were an enemy. In a sudden show of independence that startled me, he warned me that if I wished to remain his friend, I should never speak to him that way again. I was astonished and shaken up by his outburst, but concealed my feelings until he should convalesce to a state of health sufficient for me to deal with him and "set him straight." But he was snatched away from my rantings and placed in your keeping for my future consolation. Within a few days the fever returned, and at a moment when I was absent from his bedside, he died.

My heart was now darkened by grief, and everywhere I looked I saw death. My native haunts became a scene of torture to me, and my own home a misery. Without him everything we had done together turned into an excruciating ordeal. My eyes kept looking for him without finding him. I hated all the places where we used to meet, because they could no longer say to me, "Look, here he comes," as they once did. I became a problem to myself and kept asking, "Why are you cast down, O my soul, and why are you disquieted within me?" [19] But my soul didn't know what to answer. If I added the words, "Hope thou in God," [20] then my soul quite properly refused to comply. Why should it hope in God? The man my soul had loved and lost was far more real and valuable than any fantasy such as I proposed to trust. Only tears were sweet to me, and only tears were able to take the place my friend had filled in my heart's delight.

5

But now, Lord, all these things lie in the past, and time has healed my wound. Let me listen to you who are the Truth. Let the ears of my heart move closer to your mouth, so you can tell me why tears are so sweet to those in misery. Have you, who are present everywhere, placed our troubles out of your reach? You reside within yourself, but we ricochet from one rugged experience to another; and if we weren't able to pour our troubles into your ears, what hope would be left us? How can there be such a sweet flavor in the bitter fruit we pluck from life—with all its groans, tears, sighs, and wailings? Does the sweetness come from the hope that you will hear us? In the case of prayer I would say Yes, for prayer is built on a longing to get through to you. But is it also the case when one is overwhelmed by grief and anguish over something lost, as I was? (I had no hope of my friend's coming back to life; in all my weeping I never once looked for it. I just grieved and let the tears fall, for my joy had disappeared and I was heartbroken.) Or is it that weeping is a bitter thing that gives us pleasure only because it relieves the tension created by sorrow?

6

Why speak of it now? This is not the time to ask questions but, rather, to confess to you. I was a dismal mess, along with every other soul who is chained to the things of this life. When we lose these things we're all torn to pieces; then we realize we were miserable even while we had them. That's the way it was with me. I wept bitterly and found release in bitterness. Wretched as I was, I could still put my own life ahead of my friend's on whose account I felt so wretched. For while I would gladly have changed my life, I was not about to lose it even for him. Whether or not it's true, they say that Orestes and Pylades were ready to die for each other, together, because each of them held life to be worse than death without each other.[21] I felt exactly the opposite. It was a weird kind of sensation; I was fed up with living and very much afraid of dying. I suppose it was because of my great love for him that I hated and feared death as the cruel enemy that had stolen him away from me. I imagined that death would suddenly destroy all men as it had destroyed him. I still remember thinking that way.

Look into my heart, my God, look deeply into it. Notice the things that I remember. You are my hope; you cleanse me of impure motives such as these. "My eyes are ever toward the Lord, for he will pluck my feet out of the net."[22] I marveled that other mortals kept on living when he was dead, for I had loved him as though he would never die. I marveled even more that I could go on living with him dead. Someone has correctly described a friend as being "the soul's other half."[23] I felt that my soul and my friend's soul were one, but we happened to be living in two bodies; and my life became a horrible thing to me because I didn't want to live as half a soul.

7

What do you think of a madness that doesn't know enough to love men for what they are—men? What do you think of a simpleminded man who can't take what every man has to put up with? I raved, I sighed, I wept, and it became so distracting that I was unable to rest or even think. I could find no place to lay down the burden of my cut-up and bleeding soul. Neither in pleasant woods and fields, nor in laughter and music, nor in the fragrance of a garden, nor in the pomp and conviviality of banqueting, nor in the voluptuous delights of the bed and couch, nor even in books and poetry could I find rest. I hated everything, even the light itself; and when my soul finally stopped its crying, a heavy burden of misery kept it depressed.

To you, Lord, my soul should have been lifted, for I know you could have taken care of it. But I had neither the strength nor the will-power to do it. What made my situation even more trying was that I couldn't conceive of you as something firm and solid. I had some kind of empty fantasy that wasn't you at all, and so my error became my god. If I tried to unload my burden and rest it on that, it simply fell through and landed on me again. I couldn't stand my life, yet I couldn't escape it. Where could my heart go to hide from itself? Where could I go to leave myself behind? Where would I not follow myself? But I did finally leave the place of my birth. I found my eyes weren't always unconsciously searching for my missing friend if I went to places where they weren't used to seeing him. So I left the town of Thagaste and came to Carthage.

8

Time never takes time off. As it rolls on its deliberate way it affects our senses and does strange things to our minds. The days came and went, one after another, and they introduced me to other hopes and fresh memories. Little by little my soul was patched up as I resumed the kind of pleasures I had once enjoyed. The heartache began to ease and the place of sadness was occupied not by other sorrows, but by the cause of future sorrows. Why had that first great grief so easily pierced me to the quick, if it weren't that I had poured out my soul on the sand by loving a mortal as though he were immortal? What renewed and refreshed me was the consolation of other friends, with whom I went on loving the things I had formerly loved instead of you. I mean in particular the enormous myth, the bald-faced lie which our minds listened to with itching ears,[24] and which corrupted us with its adulterous message. But as far as I was concerned that religious fable would not die the way some of my friends did.

In Carthage I was charmed by the company of new friends. I loved the talk, the laughter, the courteous little gestures toward one another, the sharing of the study of books of eloquence, the companionship that was sometimes serious and sometimes hilariously nonsensical, the differences of opinion that left no more bad feeling than if a man were disagreeing with his own self, the rare disputes that simply seasoned the normal consensus of agreement. We took turns listening to each other and teaching each other. We became restless if one of us was absent, and happily welcomed him back with open arms. These are the signs of genuine affection between friends who love and are loved in return. They can be recognized through the facial expression, the tongue, the eyes, and a thousand different motions and gestures. And by those signs our souls were kindled into a blaze and melted and fused together as one.

9

This is what we like to see in our friends. We like it so much that we have a guilty conscience if we don't respond to those who love us by loving them, without asking anything else in return. That is why we feel so distressed over a friend's death, and become gloomy and 'sad. Such an occasion turns joy into bitterness so that the heart is steeped in tears, and life becomes a total loss—a living death because of the death of the living. Oh, happy is the man who loves you, my God, and his friend in you, and his enemy because of you. Such a man is the only person who never loses those who are dear to him, for they are all beloved in you, our God, and you are the God who is never lost. You made heaven and earth and fill them with your presence—for it was by filling them that you made them.[25] The only way a man can lose you is to leave you; and if he leaves you, where does he go? He can run only from your pleasure to your wrath. Where does he end up without finding your law fulfilled in his punishment? Your law is the truth and you are truth.

10

"Turn us again, O God of hosts, and cause thy face to shine, and we shall be saved." [26] Whichever way the soul of man turns, it bumps into trouble unless it turns to you. Even though the things of life that attract it are beautiful, if they are outside you and outside the soul, they spell misery. Such things wouldn't even exist if they didn't come from you. Like the sun, they rise and set; not all reach old age, but all perish. When they rise they are put on course for the duration of their existence, and the faster they reach its crest, the faster they wither and die. That's the way it goes. You made them that way because they are parts of a whole. They don't all exist at once, but some are coming as others are going; and so they make up the whole universe of which they are but parts.

Our use of language follows the same rule. We hear the individual sounds of speech, one after another, but the mind is directed to the whole sentence from the start. My soul praises you for all these things, God, because you created them all; but don't let me become stuck to them with the glue of physical attraction. They run out their course and that's the end. If the soul loves these things and insists on staying with them, it will only be ripped to pieces by unhealthy forces. There is no rest here, for the appeal of the physical does not last. It passes out of the picture, and who can chase it when it slips beyond the reach of our senses? Who, for that matter, can really grasp it while it is here and present? The physical sense is slow because it is physical sense, and is limited by its own character. It is good enough for its purpose, but it cannot stop the swift movement of all things from their appointed beginning to their appointed end. In your Word, by which they were created, they hear their fate: "Thus far and no farther!"

11

Watch your vanity level, my soul. Don't let your pride stir up such a commotion that it deafens the ear of your heart. Listen! The Word is calling you to return. Here is a place of undisturbed rest where love never deserts a man unless he deserts it first.

In this life one thing passes away and another takes its place, so that the whole material universe is composed of its various parts. "But do I ever pass away?" asks the Word of God. Build your home in him, my soul. Are you becoming fed up with lies? Then turn over everything you have to him; whatever truth has given you, commend it to the truth and you can't lose. Everything in you that has decayed will blossom again, and everything sick will be made well, and everything about your body that is perishable will be reshaped and renovated and put back together. When it dies, it will not drag you down with it to the grave, for you will stand and you will live before God, who stands and abides forever.

Why turn around and follow your flesh? Why not, rather, turn in the right direction and let it follow you? Whatever you experience through the senses is only part of the picture; you like it all right, but you don't know the whole, and the whole gives far more delight than the separate parts could ever do. Far better than these is our God, who made it all, and who cannot die because there is no one to take his place.

12

If physical objects appeal to you, [my soul,] praise God for them, but let your love revert to the one who made them, so that in pleasing yourself you don't displease him. If you have a love for souls, love them in God, because by themselves they are unstable, but in him they are solidly established. Either that or they disappear and perish. So let them be loved in him, and win as many souls to him as you can.

[My soul,] say to them [my fellow men]: "Let us love God, for he created all of us, and he is not far away. He did not create the souls of men in order to go away and leave them, for they are of him and in him. Tell me, where does truth taste sweet? In the inner heart; but unfortunately the heart has wandered away from him. Go back to your heart, you double-dealing cheat, and hang onto him who made you. Stand with him and you will stand fast. Rest in him and you will find peace. What are you doing wandering about in the rough terrain? Where do you think you're going? All the good things you love come from God, but they are pleasant and good only as they relate to him. Once your love deserts him, things rightly turn sour, because anything from God is improperly loved if it causes men to desert him. What's the point of your forever walking the steep and rocky path? There is no rest where you are hunting for it. You look and look, but it's just not where you're looking. You look for life and happiness in the land of death, but it is nowhere to be found. How can there be a happy life where there is no life at all?

"That is why our Life [27] came down here to earth and took away our death. He killed death with the sheer abundance of his own life, while calling us back to himself with thunder in his voice. He came from the Virgin's womb where our humanity was joined to him so that our mortal flesh might not be forever mortal. He came out like a bridegroom from his wedding canopy, exulting like a strong man to run a race.[28] He wasted no time but sped on his way, shouting to us by words, acts, death, life, descent, ascent—in all these ways calling us to return to him. He disappeared before our eyes that we might turn to our hearts and find him there. He left us and behold, he is here. He would not stay with us and yet he never parted from us. He returned to the place he had not moved from, since 'the world was made by him'; [29] but he was in the world, and he came into the world, to save sinners.[30] My soul confesses to him and he heals me, for I have sinned against him.[31]

"Sons of men, why are you so heavy hearted? Now that Christ the Life has descended to you, why don't you ascend with him and start living? On the other hand, how can you climb any higher when you are already standing on the summit and setting your mouth against heaven? [32] First you will have to come down that you may make your way back up, this time climbing to God. For you have been climbing against God, not toward him, and you have fallen on your faces."

Tell this to the souls you bring with you, my soul, and let them do their weeping in the valley of tears. Then you will be able to take them with you to God, because it is by his Spirit that you speak to them, if when you speak you burn with the fire of love.

13

But all this I didn't know then, because I was in love with a lower form of beauty, and as a result I hit bottom. To my friends I would put the question, "Do we love anything that isn't beautiful? Then what is beautiful? And what is beauty? What entices and wins us over to the things we love? For unless there was something splendid and beautiful about them, they would hardly attract us." And the more I observed these things, the more clearly I saw that there was a distinction between the beauty of a thing in itself, and the beauty that is found in a happy, apt relationship between different things. An example of the latter would be the way a body relates to its parts, and a shoe to a foot, and so on. And this consideration welled up in my mind out of the depth of my heart, so that I wrote a book on the subject, *Beauty and Harmony*, in two or three volumes I believe. You know how many there were, Lord, but it has slipped my memory. I no longer have them, for somehow they have become lost.

14

Lord my God, what was it that moved me to dedicate my book to Hierius, the Roman orator? I didn't even know him by sight, though I had admired his distinguished reputation for scholarship, and was much impressed by what I had heard he had said. I was even impressed by the high opinion in which he was held by others. People were amazed that a man born in Syria and trained in the Greek language should develop into such a fluent and eloquent speaker in Latin, and become so knowledgeable of things related to philosophy. Thus does a man win praise and admiration even at long range! Can it be that love passes from the mouth of the orator into the heart of the listener? Literally speaking that is absurd, but it's true that enthusiasm is contagious. We are attracted to a man who is praised if we are convinced that the person praising him is not putting us on; that is to say, that he really loves the man he is praising.

So it was that I loved men on the basis of other men's judgment and not yours, my God, by which no man is fooled. But I did not love Hierius for qualities I might have admired in a famous charioteer or a gladiator who was popular with the crowd. I admired such heroes in a very different way and for more significant reasons, for I praised them in the way I wanted others to praise me. Yet I had no desire to be praised and liked as actors are, though I liked actors and was not above praising them myself. The fact is I would prefer to be a complete unknown than to be forced to put up with their kind of fame. I would rather be hated than loved as they are.

Now, how can one soul hold all these divergent and conflicting viewpoints in balance? Just because a man likes a horse, that doesn't mean he wants to be a horse. Can't I admire something in an actor even though I don't care to become one? But an actor is a man, not a horse; and man himself is a great deep whose hairs you, Lord, have numbered,[33] so that not one is lost without your knowledge. It is easier to count the hairs on a man's head than the moods and affections of his heart.

So while that orator was the kind of man I liked and wanted to emulate, my swelled-headedness blew me off course and caused me to be "carried about with every wind."[34] Yet somehow you were secretly steering the ship all the time. Today I know, and I'm perfectly frank to confess to you, Lord, that I admired Hierius more for the applause that came his way than for the things people commended in him. How do I know this? If they had criticized him instead of praising, and had repeated the same words but used an inflection of scorn and disapproval, my enthusiasm would never have been so keen. Obviously a human soul that fails to hold to the solid rock of truth will find itself laid out flat and helpless. Those who think they know everything blow off and fill the air with words, and the soul is caught in the slipstream and sways this way and that, forward and backward, till the light is fogged over and the truth can't be found. Yet there it was right in front of us all the time!

It seemed terribly important to me that my writing and my studies be brought to the attention of this man. Had he approved of my work, I would have glowed with the thrill of it; and had he disapproved, my proud heart would have been deeply wounded, because it lacked any knowledge of your dependable guidelines. But I had a good time working on my survey of *Beauty and Harmony*, which I inscribed to him; and even though nobody else praised it, I liked it myself.

15

I failed to see that the cardinal point in any discussion of beauty and harmony is that *you* made it all. You are the Omnipotence "who only doeth wondrous things." [36] My mind was moving in the direction of physical forms. The beautiful I defined and distinguished as that which contains beauty in itself, the harmonious as that which acquires beauty through its relation to certain other things. I used physical examples to illustrate the premise. I also turned my attention to the nature of the soul, but the false opinions I held of spiritual matters blocked me from seeing the truth, even though the truth was forcing itself into my line of vision. So I switched from a consideration of disembodied subjects to matters of line and color and shape; and since I could detect no such characteristics in the soul, I decided that the soul could not be seen.

Furthermore, since I loved the peace that virtue brings and hated the discord caused by corruption and falsehood, I saw unity in the former and divisiveness in the latter. It seemed to me that this unity was composed of the rational mind, the nature of truth, and the supreme good; while in the divisiveness I imagined there was a vital principle of irrationality, plus a supreme evil that was not just substance but had a life of its own. Yet in my state of wretched ignorance I did not consider this evil to be derived from you, my God, of whom are "all things." [36] I called the unity a "monad," a kind of sexless mind, and the disunity a "dyad" which leads to crimes against others and sexual degeneracy. But I didn't know what I was talking about, because nobody had taught me that evil was not a real substance, or that man's reason is not the supreme and unchanging good.

Violent acts against other people are committed when the soul is driven by vicious and arrogant attitudes that wind out of control. Sins of self-corruption are committed, on the other hand, when all restraints are lifted from the inner drives of the soul, and it is flushed down the drain by erotic sensual behavior. In the same way, if the rational mind becomes corrupted it gives off erroneous views and false judgments that can only poison life; and that was the way it was with me. I was unaware that my mind had to be illuminated by another Light if it were to share the truth—since it was not itself the essence of truth. "For thou wilt light my candle: the Lord my God will enlighten my darkness," [37] and "from [your] fulness have all we received." [38] You are "the true Light, which lighteth every man that cometh into the world," [39] because in you there "is no variableness, neither shadow of turning." [40]

But while I was struggling toward you, you pushed me back so that I might taste of death, for "God resists the proud." [41] And what could be prouder than my sublimely foolish assertion that I was made of the same stuff that you are? I knew that I was subject to change, because I wanted to learn more and to improve myself. So I preferred to think that you, too, are changeable, rather than believe that I was not as you are. That is what pushed me back: you kept rebuffing my conceited obstinacy. So my imagination went on toying with material concepts, my flesh blamed my flesh, and my spirit became "a wind that passeth away," [42] unable to return to you. In my wanderings I drifted toward fanciful concepts of non-existent things which I invented out of physical data.

When I came across your faithful servants (my fellow citizens of the Kingdom from which I, in my ignorance, stood exiled),[43] I would blab away to them with such stupid remarks as, "If God made the soul, why did he permit it to make mistakes?" But I didn't allow anyone to come back at me with, "Why does God himself make mistakes?" I preferred to contend that your unchangeable character was forced into error by necessity, rather than admit that my own changeable character deviated from the truth of its own free will so that what started out as my error became my punishment.

I was twenty-six or twenty-seven years old when I wrote that book. My mind carefully examined the different qualities of the sensory impressions that were dinning at the ears of my heart; and all the while I was straining to catch your inner melody, beloved Truth. I meditated on *Beauty and Harmony*, but I really longed to be "the bridegroom's friend, who stands by and listens to him, [and] is overjoyed at hearing the bridegroom's voice." [44] But I couldn't. The voices of my own error snatched me away, and I was plummeted downward by the weight of my pride. You would neither "fill me with joy and gladness" [45] nor "let the bones which thou hast broken rejoice." [46]

16

When I was just twenty years old there came into my hands Aristotle's treatise on the *Ten Categories*.[47] My master of rhetoric at Carthage and other teachers had acclaimed this book, mouthing its title with their cheeks puffed out in pride, so that I now looked upon the name "Aristotle" as though gaping at some kind of great and divine mystery. However, once I got into it I was able to read and master it by myself—though today I wonder why I bothered. On checking with other students I learned that they had a hard time understanding it even with the help of the finest teachers, who not only lectured but drew diagrams for them in the sand. I found they couldn't tell me anything about it that I had not already discovered in my own reading.

The book's meaning seemed clear to me. It defined substances, such as man, and the "accidents" or attributes of a substance, such as the shape of a man, which is its *quality*; the height of a man in feet, which is *quantity*; also, *relation* to other things, such as a man's relationship to his brother; and *position*, such as his status, and *where* and *when* he was born, and whether he is standing or sitting. It identified *possessions* as one attribute, whether he wears shoes or bears arms. It also defined *what he does* and *what is done to him*. I have mentioned these examples of the nine categories and the chief category of substance; but I could have included countless others under those headings.

What did all this profit me? Nothing; actually it held me back. I tried to understand you, my God (who are so marvelously uncomplicated and unchangeable), by forcing everything in the world into Aristotle's ten categories. Imagine thinking of you as a "substance" and of your greatness and beauty as "attributes" as they would be in a body. The truth is that your greatness and your beauty are yourself! A body is not necessarily great or beautiful because it is a body; were it not so great or beautiful it would still be a body. My conception of you was unsound, false, a figment of my misery, and hardly a solid foundation for your gift of happiness. You ordered the earth to bring forth thorns and thistles for me, and it did. You ordered me to eat bread in the sweat of my face—and I did.[48]

What did it profit me to read all the books I could find in the so-called liberal arts when I had become a person of no character, a dropout from society and a sex addict? I enjoyed the books, but I had no clue as to the source of such truth and certitude as they contained. I had my back to the light and my face toward the things it illuminated; but my face, which could see what was in the light, remained in the darkness. It was not hard for me to understand whatever I read in the fields of rhetoric, logic, geometry, music, or arithmetic, even without instruction. You know this, Lord my God, because keenness of perception and quickness of intelligence are your gifts; but I failed to lay them on your altar. As a result, they did not help me but, rather, helped to destroy me. I struggled to keep to myself a large part of the substance you placed in my keeping, and did not put my strength and power in custody for you; rather, I left you and went wandering into a far country,[49] where I squandered your gifts by responding to the bewitchment of the local trollops.

What good was this ability if I made no use of it? Actually I didn't realize my ability, because I was not aware that these subjects were difficult until I tried explaining them and found that the best of my students could only follow my explanations slowly. But of what value was it all to me, Lord God of truth, so long as I considered you to be an immense body of radiation and myself a piece of you? What a fallacy! Yet that's the way it was, my God, and I don't blush to confess to you openly the mercies you have shown me, or to call on you for help, any more than I blushed at that time to spell out my blasphemies openly before men, and to bark at you like a dog.

What was the value of my cleverness, which moved so easily through all these studies and unraveled so many knotty questions without the aid of human teachers? Because all the while I was trapped in the worst error of all: a shameful and ugly profaning of the life of devotion to you. I can't see that it was such a roadblock to your faithful ones [50] that they were somewhat slower than I in mental power. They didn't desert you. They remained safely in the nest of your church, where their plumes grew and their wings of love were strengthened on the food of a healthy faith.

O Lord our God, "in the shadow of your wings" [51] give us hope. Protect us and sustain us. Hold us up. Hold us up as infants and hold us up as gray-haired old men. When you are our strength we are strong; when our strength is our own we are helpless. With you our good is lasting and permanent; when we turn from you, our aversion becomes a perversion. Let it be that we might return to you, Lord, and not be overturned. With you our good lives on, free of defect, because it is you yourself. If we fail to maintain our earthly homes they fall into ruin, but it's not so of the soul's home, which is your eternity.

BOOK FIVE

A Barque to Italy

1

Lord, you made my tongue and you moved it to confess your name. Now accept the sacrifice of praise it offers to you. Heal all my bones so they will say, "Lord, who in the world is like you?" [1] The locked-up heart cannot keep you out. No matter how hard and stiff a man's heart may be, it cannot resist the touch of your hand. You unlock it whenever you wish, whether for mercy or for justice—"and there is nothing hid from the heat thereof." [2] But let my soul praise you so it may love you, and let it tell your mercy so it may praise you. All the creatures of your universe join in an unending chorus of praise: The spirit of man does it by the word of his mouth to you, and the animals and inanimate nature express themselves through the mouth of him who observes them. When our souls become depressed, they find sympathetic support in the things you have created, and so are lifted up to you, the marvelous Creator of everything. Thus by you are we made anew and given access to the source of courage.

2

Let the vagabonds roam and the evildoers try to escape from you; your eye still follows them and picks them out among the shadows. The whole universe is filled with beauty, except for those people who pollute it. And where do they go? When they run from your face, where can't you go to find them? Obviously the wicked do not realize that you are everywhere, that you are not circumscribed by spatial limitations. You alone are present even to those who try to get as far away from you as they can.

Let them turn around and look at you. They may have deserted their Creator, but you have not deserted your creatures. Let them turn and discover you are in their hearts, in the hearts of all those who, after traveling that old rocky road, confess you and throw themselves at your feet and weep on your breast, and find you gently wiping away their tears.[3] That discovery may make them weep all the more, but now they are weeping tears of joy, because it is not some person of flesh and blood but *you*, Lord, the One who created them, who makes them into new creations and gives them the kind of encouragement they need.

And where was I all the time I was looking for you? You were right there before me, but I was running away from myself. I couldn't even find myself, much less you.

3

I call up for inspection before my God the twenty-ninth year of my life. A Manichean bishop named Faustus arrived in Carthage, a devil's bait who managed to trap many people by the charm of his eloquence. At first I too was taken in by him, but I was beginning to discern the truth from the mere form of it. I had no interest in the dish Faustus was using to serve up his fare, but I took the keenest interest in the kind of food he was preparing. By reputation he was an expert in all the major branches of higher learning and was especially skilled in the discipline of the humanities. I had read some books on astronomy and natural philosophy, and still retained much of what I'd studied. When I was comparing these scientific writings with the farfetched fables of the Manicheans, it seemed to me that the scientists had the better of it, for they were able to think clearly enough to form a fair judgment of the universe, even though they could not penetrate through to its sovereign Lord.

That is because such men fall into pride. They accurately predict an eclipse of the sun, then fall into a state of eclipse themselves. They neglect to investigate the source of the intelligence by which they conduct their research. They do not know the Way. They do not know your incarnate Word, by whom you made all the things that are numbered, including those who do the numbering and the brains they use to number. Your wisdom is beyond all such measuring and numbering,[4] but your only begotten Son was "made our wisdom, our righteousness and sanctification and redemption." [5] He was numbered among us,[6] and paid his taxes to Caesar.[7]

They do not know the Way by which they can descend from their self-imagined loftiness to him, and then by him ascend to him. They do not know this Way, but consider themselves so high and mighty that they shine among the stars. Unfortunately such people plunge to earth and their senseless minds become darkened.[8] Much of what the natural philosophers and scientists are saying about the created universe is true, but they show no interest in a devout search for the Truth who put the universe together. So they fail to find him; or if they do find him, they do "not honor him as God or give thanks to him," but instead become "futile in their thinking," and "claiming to be wise," they attribute to themselves what is really yours, projecting (by an eager but perverted loss of insight) their own qualities onto you. They even go so far as to attribute lies to you who are the Truth. They exchange "the glory of the immortal God for images resembling mortal men or birds or animals or reptiles," and further exchange "the truth about God for a lie," in order to worship and serve "the creature rather than the Creator."

6

So for nearly nine years, while listening more or less irresolutely to the Manichean teaching, I had looked forward to the long-awaited arrival of this man Faustus. Other Manichees whom I happened to meet had failed to answer my questions, but invariably promised me that when Faustus appeared he would sit down with me and explain not only these answers, but the answers to any other questions I might raise.

At last he came, and I found him to be a pleasant person with a delightful manner of speech. He talked in the usual Manichean way, but with far more personality than the others. In my state of thirst, however, I was not too fussy about the refinement of the cupbearer or the costly value of his cup. My ears had already been dinned to death by such stuff as he taught. Just because it was expressed in better grammar didn't make it sound any better, nor did it ring truer because it was more eloquent. I was aware that a handsome face and becoming speech did not guarantee a wise mind, and that those who promised me wisdom on such a basis misjudged the evidence.

But my eagerness to meet the long-awaited Faustus was more than rewarded by the congenial attitude in which he approached disputation and the language he used to clothe his thoughts. Because I was so charmed by him, I praised him along with the others—probably more than the others did. At the first opportunity I, with some of my friends, began to besiege his ears, and when the time seemed right we involved Faustus in a discussion. I mentioned some matters to him that disturbed me, but quickly learned that his knowledge of the liberal arts was nonexistent, and even his literary skill was of the superficial kind common to public speakers. He had read some of Cicero's orations, a very few of Seneca's books, a bit of poetry, and some of the Latin writings of the Manicheans. These along with his daily speaking schedule gave him a certain command of language, which was made more acceptable by his appealing personal magnetism and the good use he made of his intellectual powers.

7

After it became apparent to me that Faustus was really ignorant in those fields in which I thought he was strong, I began to lose hope of getting any clarifying answers from him to the problems that bothered me. I wanted the man to show me that the explanations of the Manichees were better than, or at least as good as, the astronomical calculations about the heavens and the stars and the sun and the moon that I had studied elsewhere. Now I realized that he was unable to supply any such explanations. When I asked him to consider these matters and discuss them with me, he modestly excused himself from the task. I liked him better for it, because the mind that honestly admits its limitations is more attractive than that which simply reaches out for knowledge. I found him reacting in a similar way to all the more subtle and difficult questions that came to him.

The zeal I had acquired for Manichean studies was frustrated by this encounter. Once I got to know Faustus well, all my plans to advance in the teachings of his religion fell apart. I did not separate myself entirely from the Manichees because I couldn't seem to find anything else, so I chose to stay with them until something better turned up. Faustus, who had been such a deadly snare [9] to many, now began without knowing it to release me from the jaws of the trap in which I was caught. For your hand, my God, in the mystery of your Providence, did not desert my soul. Night and day my mother prayed for me to you through her tears, and you dealt with me in a marvelous way. It was you who guided me, my God, for "it is the Lord who directs a man's steps, he holds him firm and watches over his path." [10] What else but your hand is able to save us by remaking what it has made?

8

You brought such pressure to bear on me that I was persuaded to go to Rome and teach there the subjects I had been teaching in Carthage. It was not my friends' assurance of higher fees and greater recognition that prompted me to go to Rome, although those considerations carried weight of course. The main reason was I had heard that Roman students were quieter and discipline was stricter. At Carthage, by contrast, the students are completely out of control and take disgraceful liberties. They invade the classroom like a pack of maniacs, and commit all kinds of reckless acts that ought to be punished by law, were it not that custom protects them. Your eternal law, however, will never sanction such antics, and in the long run the students only hurt themselves.

As a student I had been unwilling to join in such behavior, but now as a teacher I was forced to put up with it in others. That was why I was glad to go to a place where, as I was told, such things were not allowed. But the truth is, you are "my refuge and my portion in the land of the living," [11] and you goaded me into leaving Carthage and going to another country so you could save my soul. You held out enticements that would lure me, and secretly used my own contrariness—and that of my friends—to bring it off.

You knew, God, why I left one city and went to the other, but you neglected to inform either me or my mother. You whipped her with the rod of sorrow, and properly so, for her too-carnal longing to be with me. She was acutely upset over my leaving, and followed me right down to the water's edge, determined either to bring me home or to go with me. But I lied to her, saying I had a friend on board the ship with whom I wished to spend some time before it sailed. After persuading her to spend the night at a nearby chapel erected in memory of Cyprian, I went back and slipped aboard. The wind came up and filled our sails, and the Mediterranean shoreline dropped away. My mother discovered the deception next day. After weeping and lamenting in your ears and rebuking me for my cruelty, she managed to get over it and resumed her prayers for me. She returned home and I went on to Rome.

9

At Rome I came down with a severe illness and very nearly went to my eternal judgment, carrying with me all the sins I had committed against you, against others, and against myself, over and above the bondage of original sin through which we have all died with Adam. You had not yet forgiven me those sins in Christ, nor had he, on the cross, dissolved the enmity that my sins had incurred in your sight. How could the crucifixion of a phantom (which is what I believed happened at Calvary) loose me from my sins? But despite my soul's danger I still had no desire to be baptized at the time. As a sick boy I had been a better person, for I had begged my mother to let me be baptized; but I had grown more callous with the years.

10

Eventually you healed my sickness. You restored bodily health to the son of your maidservant, so that he might live to receive a far better and sounder kind of health. In Rome I kept up my contacts with the Manicheans, for I was still convinced that it was not we who sinned, but some other nature that sinned in us. It pleased my pride to maintain that I was not to blame, so that when I did do something wrong, I would not have to confess it by saying, "Heal my soul; for I have sinned against you." [12] I loved to excuse myself and to blame this other "thing" that was in me but was not myself. The truth was that it was all myself, every bit of it, and my divided nature had been brought about simply by my wickedness. My sin was all the harder to heal because I did not consider myself a sinner.

At the same time I had given up hope of profiting from the Manichean doctrine. It occurred to me that the philosophers whom they call "Academics" [13] seemed to know more than the others, because they held that men ought to doubt everything, and that there is no truth that can be known for certain.

While I no longer defended Manicheism with my former enthusiam, I was still on intimate terms with its followers, many of whom were harbored in Rome. Their friendship made me slow to look for another religion, especially since I had given up the prospect of ever finding truth in your church, Lord of heaven and earth, Creator of all things visible and invisible. When I tried to think of my God, I thought of a shapeless mass because I didn't know what else to think. Evil was also a mass, I imagined, but one that was coarse and ugly. And because my belief—such as it was— did not permit me to consider that the good God could create evil, I imagined that there were two material masses, both infinite, of which the good was on a larger scale and the evil somewhat smaller.

All my other wrong speculations stemmed from this one fatal mistake. When I tried to go back to the Christian faith, I reacted negatively to it because I had a distorted idea as to what the Christian faith was. I thought of our Savior, your only begotten, as vaguely projected for our salvation from the radiating mass of Deity. Any spiritually mature person will smile tolerantly at me for holding such mixed-up notions, but that's the way I was.

11

There were certain things in the Old and New Testaments that I considered impossible to defend. I wanted very much to take them up one by one with someone who knew his Bible, and to get his view of them. Even before I left Carthage I had been impressed by the public statements of a Christian named Elpidius, who would engage in debate with the Manicheans and would cite the Scriptures in a way that was not easy to refute. It seemed to me that the response of his opponents was weak. The truth is, they didn't give their real arguments in public, but mentioned them only among us in private. They believed that the Scriptures of the New Testament had been doctored by some unknown scribes who wanted to introduce the Jewish law into the Christian faith, but they couldn't produce any "undoctored" copies to prove it. But it was principally those two masses of good and evil that I choked on, because I couldn't get my thinking out of physical categories. I gasped for the clean, pure air of your truth, but was unable to breathe it.

12

I quickly got down to the business of teaching rhetoric, which was what had brought me to Rome. At first I collected some pupils in my lodgings and through them I began to become known around town. However, I discovered there were problems in Rome I had not had to put up with in Africa. I was warned that while it was true students did not riot in Rome, they had other tricks, such as cheating the teacher of his fees by suddenly transferring in a body to another master. They would renege on their good faith, since justice meant nothing to them compared with the love of money. I can't stand crooked people; yet I love them and hope to get them to change their ways, and to prefer instruction more than money, and more than anything else to love you, God, the Truth, the source of abundant goodness and virtuous peace. But in those days I was more interested in seeing that they didn't cheat me than I was in wanting them to become good for your sake.

13

A letter came from Milan to the prefect of the city of Rome, asking for a teacher of rhetoric to be sent to that city at public expense. I applied for the post through my Manichean connections. My hidden purpose was to walk out on my Manichee friends, though neither I nor they fully sensed it. The Roman prefect, Symmachus, prescribed a subject for a trial oration, and after the audition he approved me and sent me off.[14] So I came to Milan and to Ambrose, the bishop, a devout fieldhand in your vineyard who was known all over the world as one of its choicest men. In those days his great preaching gave to your people the richness of your grain, the joy of your oil, and the sober intoxication of the wine of your Spirit.[15] I was totally ignorant of course of the fact that you were leading me to him in order that he might (with full knowledge) lead me to you.

This man of God received me in a fatherly way and, as a good bishop should, he told me he was delighted that I had come from abroad to stay in Milan. So I came to love Ambrose, not at that time as a teacher of truth (which I had given up hope of ever finding in your church) but as a man who was friendly and kind. I went to church and listened to him when he preached to the people—not with the intent I should have shown, but just to see whether I thought his eloquence was all it was reputed to be, and whether it flowed in a greater or lesser degree than I had been led to expect. I hung upon his words intently; but as for the subject matter, I found it dull and even contemptible. The charm of his

delivery pleased me, even though it seemed less soothing and capti-
vating than Faustus'. Ambrose was the better educated of the two
men, and of course I am referring only to their manner of speaking.
From every other viewpoint there was no comparison between
them. Faustus meandered among the fallacies of the Manicheans,
while Ambrose taught a healthy gospel of salvation. But salvation
is far from the wicked,[16] which is what I was when I came to
Milan. Even so without knowing it I was gradually drawing closer.

14

As I indicated, I took no notice of what Ambrose said, but only
of the way he said it. Elocution was the only drab interest left
to me, now that I had lost hope of man's ever finding his way to
you. Nevertheless as my mind listened to the words (which I admired), it could not avoid their meaning (which I preferred to
ignore). So while my heart was open to what Ambrose could teach
me about eloquence, I began at the same time gradually to absorb
the truth of what he was saying. For the first time it seemed to me
that his arguments could be defended, and that the Christian
faith, which I had thought could not stand up against the Manichean attacks, could reasonably be maintained on its own grounds.
But I did not yet feel that I should follow the Christian way just
because some learned doctors were defending its position and
answering objections with a show of sense. Nor did I think my
own ideas should be damned when both viewpoints were equally
defensible. For it seemed to me that the Christian position, while
it had not been demolished, was still far from being victorious.

If I could have conceived of a spiritual substance, all the con-
trived arguments of the Manicheans would have immediately
fallen flat; but it just was not possible. As I continued to analyze
the physical world and the natural order, as apprehended through
the senses, it seemed to me that for the most part the philosophers

were probably right. So I deemed it wise to adopt the supposed habit of the Academics of doubting everything. I wavered between such opinions until finally I decided to leave the Manicheans, for it didn't seem proper to remain with them while preferring the views of the philosophers. Yet I took exception to the idea of entrusting my puny soul into the care of the philosophers, since they ignored entirely the saving name of Christ. So as long as I was a neophyte under instruction in the Christian church, and had been since my parents urged me to become one, I decided to stay that way until some kind of certainty came through, by which I might direct my course.

BOOK SIX

Locked in Immortal Combat

1

Where were you all this time, Hope of my youth? Why were you hiding? Did you not teach me more than the beasts of the earth, and make me wiser than the fowls of heaven? [1] Yet I kept walking on dark and slippery trails and searching for you outside of myself, while failing to find the God of my own heart. I went right down into the ocean abyss and stayed there, because I despaired of ever discovering the truth.

By now my mother had come to join me in Milan. Her love had given her the courage to cross land and sea, and when she found herself in danger she simply sought her safety in you. On one occasion as the ship on which she was crossing from Africa seemed about to sink, it was she who put valor into the hearts of the sailors rather than vice versa. She told them there was no question that they would land safely, because you had promised it to her in a vision—and they did.

When Mother reached Milan I informed her that while I was not a Christian, neither was I any longer a Manichean. She seemed unimpressed. Quietly she witnessed to me out of a confident heart of her faith in Christ, and predicted that before she left this life she would see me a believer. She went regularly to the church, where she hung upon the words of Ambrose as "a well of water springing up into everlasting life." [2] She loved that man and looked

upon him as an angel of God, because she knew it was by him I
had been brought to my current state of wobbling uncertainty.

2

As I have suggested, it was because my salvation was at stake
that she loved Ambrose greatly, and he loved her because of her
fervent life of devotion, which took the form of good works and
frequent churchgoing. Sometimes when he saw me he would
break out in praise of her and congratulate me on having such a
mother—not knowing what a son she had! For I was one who now
doubted everything, and was convinced the road that leads to life
cannot be found.

3

During this period I did not wrestle in prayer, asking you to
come to my help. Instead I was forever popping off with questions,
restlessly eager for an argument. Measuring Ambrose by worldly
standards, I reckoned him a lucky man because he was honored
by so many important people. As to what hopes he carried with
him, what temptations were incident to his high station, what was
his comfort in times of trouble, and what his joy when his heart
secretly fed upon your bread—of these things I knew nothing and
had no way of knowing.

At the same time Ambrose himself knew nothing of the emotional excitement I was going through or the spiritual traps that
were ensnaring me. I couldn't talk to him the way I wanted to
because of the hordes of people coming to see him. They kept
him so busy with their problems that I was never able to get in to
him either to talk or to listen. I had no chance to ask the many
questions that I wanted to put to this holy oracle of yours, unless

it was something that he could take just a moment to listen to. For me to spill my problems in his ear was going to require lots of time, and that Ambrose never seemed to have. Yet every Lord's Day as I listened to him rightly dividing the word of truth to the people,[3] I became more and more convinced that all the knotty questions and clever attacks directed by deceiving men against the Holy Scriptures could be resolved and answered.

I found out that your spiritual sons who are regenerated through Grace do not take the phrase, "God created man in his own image," [4] to mean that you are limited to the shape of a human body. I had not the faintest or foggiest notion of what a "spiritual substance" was at the time; yet I was happy to make the discovery, embarrassing as it was, that I had been ranting all those years not against the Christian faith but against some figment of the imagination. I had been thoughtlessly and irreverently making accusations without doing my research.

4

But it often happens that a man who has had a bad doctor is afraid to trust a good one. Thus my soul could not find its way back to a state of health except by believing; and rather than believe what was false, I refused the cure. I resisted your hands that prepared the medicine of faith and dispensed it to the whole world with the authority to cure man's sickness.

5

From this point I began to give priority to Christian teaching, which demanded (although with moderation and honesty) that certain things be accepted on faith even though they cannot be proved. Then, Lord, your hand began to work over my heart in the gentlest and most merciful way, putting it back together. I considered the fact that I believed countless things that I had never seen, as I had not been present when they took place. The list of such things would include historical events, facts about cities and places which I had not visited, and things I took for granted on the word of friends or doctors or other people—without which belief it would be impossible to accomplish anything in this life. The list would include, too, the firm and unshakable faith which told me who my parents were—something I could never know except by believing and accepting what I had heard.

So I came to realize that it was not those who believed the Scriptures, which you have established with such authority over nearly the whole human family, but those who did not believe it, who were in error. Moreover, I was not to listen to those who might say to me, "How do you know that the Scriptures were given to the human race by the Spirit of the one true God?" because this was the one thing that I was to believe above everything else.

My belief that you exist, and that you care for us, was sometimes robust and sometimes feeble, but I always hung onto it even though I didn't know which way led to you, or what to make of your "substance." Recognizing that we men don't have the strength to discover the truth by the light of reason, and that we need the authority of Holy Scripture, I began to sense that you would never have given commanding authority to the Bible throughout the world, had it not been your will that men should seek you in it and come to faith in you. Now that I heard the Scriptures credibly expounded, I saw that those passages that had struck me as absurd belonged really to the deep mysteries of faith. The sacred authority of Scripture thus seemed to me to be heightened, since it can be read easily by anybody, yet in its deeper meanings it carries an awesome mystery. The plain language and crude style employed by the Bible make it easy to get into, but it can still tax the highest capacity of the trained mind.

6

I was anxious to get married, make money, and become famous, and you laughed at the whole business. My ambition landed me in all sorts of unpleasant situations, but you brought good out of it all, because you wouldn't let anything nice happen to me that didn't come from you. Look at my heart, Lord, for it was your idea that I pull these things out of the past and confess them to you.

One day I was putting the final touches on an oration I had to recite in praise of the emperor.[5] The piece was shot through with lies that the people would dutifully applaud, knowing all the time they were lies. I had been stewing about this problem, and the thoughts of my heart were quite feverish and agitated as I walked along a street in Milan with some friends. I noticed a beggar whom I guessed was drunk, because he was making jokes and was obviously lighthearted. The sight made me feel worse than ever, and I turned to my friends and remarked about the way our own behavior seems to pile trouble and sorrow on us. For all these strained exertions of ours, caused by the drive of ambition, were forcing us to drag a heavy load of misery; and in my case the farther I dragged it the heavier it got. Yet all our struggling was aimed at one thing: to achieve some kind of peace and joy—which our beggar had already attained, while it looked as if we never would!

Granted, he had not found true happiness—but the kind of happiness I had in mind was even more phony. At least he was enjoying himself, while I was a study in anxiety. He was carefree while I was bogged down by phobias. Yet if anyone had asked me whether I would have preferred the beggar's life to my own, I would have said No. It was no good telling me, "The difference lies in what brings happiness. The beggar found his pleasure in inebriation, you find yours in glory." What kind of glory was it,

Lord? Not yours. If the beggar didn't know true happiness, neither did I know true glory. He would sleep off his saturated condition, but I went to bed with my problem and woke up with it, went to bed with it and woke up with it, day after day.

Now at last I realize that the difference does indeed lie in what brings happiness. The joy of hope that faith brings is something that goes beyond all hollow pride. But at the time my inebriated friend had the best of me, not only because he felt hilarious while my insides were torn to pieces, but because he had got his wine by wishing luck to passersby, while I was building my ego by telling people lies.

11

I now began reflecting anxiously on the long period that had elapsed since I was nineteen years old, when I first began to take seriously the search for wisdom.[6] I had decided then that once I discovered wisdom, I would give up all the vain desires and false hopes that fed my ambitions. Being now thirty years old and stuck in the same ditch, I continued greedily to enjoy the passing pleasures of life even though they were dissipating my strength.

I would talk to myself in this manner:

"Tomorrow I will find the truth. It will become clear to me and I'll take hold of it . . .

"When Faustus comes he will explain everything . . .

"What great men those Academics are. Is it true, as they say, that there is no certainty a man can take hold of to guide him in this life . . . ?

"No, we must look harder and not give up. I know now that the Scriptures that seemed so ridiculous to me once are not really ridiculous at all. They can be understood quite honestly and intelligently in another sense . . .

"I shall set my foot on the step where my parents placed me

as a boy, until I have fully investigated the truth. . . . But where shall I find it? And when . . . ?

"Ambrose is too busy to see me and I am too busy to read. And if I did have time, where would I get the books? From whom could I buy them or borrow them? I must work out a schedule and plan my day for the well-being of my soul . . .

"I have great hopes: the Christian faith doesn't teach what I thought it did; some of my accusations are without foundation. Should I inquire further into the matter . . . ?

"My pupils take up my morning hours, but what about the rest of the day? Should I use it to study the church's teaching? Then when do I cultivate the influential friends whose approval is so important to my future? When do I prepare the lessons for which the students pay me? When do I get some recreation and relax my mind after the strain of teaching . . . ?

"Chuck the whole business. I'm going to get it out of my mind once and for all, and devote myself solely and completely to the search for truth . . .

"Life is miserable, death is inevitable, and no one knows when the end will come. Am I ready to die? Where can I learn what I have neglected here? Won't I be punished for my neglect . . . ?

"What if death puts an end to all thought and care and feeling? I must look into this. It's unthinkable that it could be so. God would never have done such great things for us if the life of the soul ended with the death of the body . . .

"Why delay then? Why not abandon all earthly hopes and apply myself to the quest for God and the joy of knowing him . . . ?

"But hold on—this life is not so bad. It has a certain charm of its own. One must not cut oneself off from its pleasures so lightly . . .

"It wouldn't be hard for me to get myself a position of preferment in the city. What more do I want? I have plenty of important connections. In a necessity, I could pick up a governorship if nothing better. If I married a wife, the dowry would bring in some money to take care of the extra expense. That's about all I would need . . ."

These things kept turning over in my mind, while the wind blew my heart first one way and then another. Time was passing, yet I kept putting off my conversion to the Lord. Day after day I postponed the decision to live in you, though I hardly put off dying daily in myself! I really wanted a happy life, yet I was afraid to look for it on its own premises; and even while I ran away from it I kept looking for it. I thought that self-discipline was something that was supposed to be achieved in our own strength, though I knew I didn't have it. I failed to realize that you would have given me this inner strength had I asked for it, and had I cast my cares on you in believing faith.[7]

13

Every effort was being made to find me a wife. I proposed to a girl and accordingly we became engaged. My mother did all she could to bring off the marriage, because she reasoned that the wedding would be followed by my baptism. She saw this as the answer to her prayers and the fulfilling of your promise to her, and was pleased that my faith seemed to be adjusting to it. The plans went forward, and the arrangement was made for marriage to this girl who was two years under the legal age.[8] I liked her all right and agreed to wait for her.

15

Meanwhile my sins kept on multiplying. The woman who shared my bed for so many years was torn from my side as an "impediment" to my forthcoming marriage; but my heart, broken and bleeding, still clung to her. She sailed back to Africa vowing she would never know another man, and leaving with me our natural son.[9] I was impatient at the prospect of a two-year delay before I could marry my intended wife, and being a slave to sex rather than a lover of marriage, I acquired another unattached female. This prolonged and renewed and aggravated the disease of my soul under the umbrella of well-established custom, and made certain that the habit would persist into the life of marriage itself. Meanwhile the wound I received from the cutting-off of my earlier affair remained unhealed. After the burning pain of grief had passed, it turned into a dull ache that rendered me increasingly hopeless.

16

In those days I often discussed with my friends Alypius and Nebridius [10] the nature of good and evil. Epicurus would have walked off with the honors, in my judgment, except for the fact that I believed that the soul survived beyond death and would be judged on its merits—which Epicurus never would have accepted.[11] I liked to say that if we were immortal and could live in perpetual enjoyment of our bodies without fear of ever losing that pleasure, it would be enough to make us happy without asking for anything more. I was so blind I did not realize that true human dignity, like beauty that is beloved for its own sake, is not discerned by the eye of flesh, but is seen only by the inward eye.

BOOK SEVEN

The Anatomy of Evil

1

My unmentionable days of adolescence were at an end. I was now in young manhood, in bad moral and spiritual shape and getting worse. As a man (such as I was) I tried to think about the one true Almighty God. From the bottom of my heart I believed you were incorruptible; that you can never be hurt; and that you never change. I couldn't explain why I believed it, but I was dead certain that something corruptible is inferior to something incorruptible. That which can be violated I also unhesitatingly put beneath that which is inviolate; and that which is unchanging I placed above that which undergoes change.

3

But while I firmly believed that you, our Lord, the true God, are free from defilement and change and are the Creator of everyone and everything, I still had difficulties with the problem of evil. But I did come to see that whatever the solution might be, it didn't help to believe that God was changeable.

I tried to understand what I had been told, that we do evil of our free will, and the suffering that results is only just and right and comes from you. Somehow I failed to get it through my head.

I tried to pull my mental process out of the rut in which it was mired, but it slipped back again and again. One thing did lift me up toward your light; as sure as I lived, I knew that I possessed a will, and that when I willed to do something or willed not to do something, nobody else was making the decision. I was at the point of perceiving that here was the cause of my sin. But when I did do something against my will, it seemed to me that it was something done to me rather than something I did. So I considered it not my fault, but rather a punishment; and since I knew you to be a just God, I had to admit that the punishment was just.

Then I would ask, "Who made me? Not my God, who is not only good but Goodness itself. For if he did, how is it I will to do evil and bypass the good, and so earn punishment for myself? Who gave me this will? Who planted this seed of bitterness in me when all I am is what God made me, and he is Sweetness itself? If the devil is to blame, where did the devil come from? Suppose the devil was a good angel who by his own contrary will became the devil, where did his evil will come from? Didn't the Creator, who is all good, make his angels all good?" I continued to be depressed and stultified by such thoughts, but at least I was not brought to the hellish state in which a man will not confess to you, but prefers to believe that you permit evil rather than that man commits it.

5

I was searching for the origin of evil, but was unaware that there was evil even in my methodology. I brought into perspective the whole universe, both that which is visible such as earth, sea, air, stars, trees, and animal life; and that which is invisible such as heaven, the angels, and spiritual beings. For I still thought of spiritual things in a physical sense, and imagined they had a geographical environment. So I made of all creation one glorious mass of bodies. It was as if there were a vast sea, and within it a sponge that was penetrated in every part by the sea. I said, "Here is God and here is what he has created. Since God is good, then that which he made is good.

"Now, where does evil come from? How did it get here? What is its root? What is its seed? Is there any such thing in fact as evil? Was there something evil in the material from which God created the universe? When he formed it, did he leave something in it that was not converted to good? If so, why? Didn't he have power to change it, since he is omnipotent? Why didn't he just annihilate it? Could it exist against his will?"

Such thoughts kept revolving in my unhappy mind, which was aggravated by the fear that I might die before I ever found the truth. Yet in my heart I still clung to faith in Christ our Lord and Savior, as the church trained me to do. I was not clear on many points and was unsound on others, but my mind didn't entirely let faith go; rather, I kept drinking in more and more day by day.

7

By now, my Helper, you had unshackled me from the chains of divination and astrology, but I was still looking for a solution to the problem of evil and finding none. My God, what torment my heart went through! How I cried out for relief! But you were there listening, unknown to me. Even when I was quiet, my silent agony became a strong voice calling for your mercy. Nobody knew the trouble I felt—nobody but you. I couldn't seem to communicate it even to my closest friends. There was no time, there were no words to share it with them. But as I "roared by reason of the disquietness of my heart," [1] all my lack was laid before you.

8

Truly, Lord, you are eternal, and you are not angry with us forever,[2] for you take pity on us who are dust and ashes. You looked
me over and were pleased to shape what was misshapen in me.
You kept on pricking at my heart, keeping me unsettled until I
could see you clearly. The secret touch of the Great Physician's
hand restored the disturbed and darkened sight of my mind's eye,
and the salve of sorrow gradually brought it to health and keenness of vision.

9

You wanted first of all to make clear to me that you oppose the
proud man but "give grace to the humble." [3] What great mercy
you showed when you took the path of humility as the Word became flesh and dwelt among men! You used an intellectual stuffed
shirt to obtain for me some of the books of the Platonists that had
been translated from Greek into Latin. I found the gospel in them
—not the exact words, but the same meaning, and wrapped in
powerful reasoning: "In the beginning was the Word, and the
Word was with God, and the Word was God. . . . All things were
made through him. . . . In him was life, and the life was the light
of men."

In those same books I learned that the soul of man testifies to
the light, yet it is not that light; that the Word, God himself, is
"the true light that enlightens every man coming into the world."
But I did not read in them that "he came to his own home, and
his own people received him not. But to all who received him,
who believed in his name, he gave power to become children of
God." In the same way I read that the Word, God, was "born,
not of blood nor of the will of the flesh nor of the will of man, but

of God." But that "the Word became flesh and dwelt among us" [4]—that I failed to find in the works of the Platonists.

The books taught me in a variety of different ways that the Son of God was divine like the Father, but neglected to add that he humbled himself and took the nature of a slave, and made himself of no reputation, and became obedient unto death, even the death of a cross.[5] They said the Son lives forever with you in eternity, but there was no word to the effect that he died for us sinners. It seems some people get so high up on their doctrinal stilts they can't hear the Lord saying, "Learn of me, for I am meek and lowly of heart, and you shall find rest for your souls." [6]

10

These Platonic writings did advise me to return to myself, and you then led me into my inner consciousness. I was able to do so because you helped me.[7] The eye of my soul—such as it was—saw the Unchanging Light shining over it. This was no ordinary light of day, visible to the naked eye; nor was it an intensifying of that light to the nth degree. It was not floating over my mind as oil floats above water, or as the sky is over the earth. Rather, it was something altogether different. It was over me because it made me, and I was beneath it because I was made by it. But everyone who knows the truth knows that Light, and he who knows it knows it forever. It is the light of love.

Eternal truth, truth of love, love of eternity! That's what you are, my God, and that's why day and night you form the breath of my being. When I first knew you, you lifted me up and I realized there was something to see, but I wasn't quite capable of seeing it. My vision was too weak to stand the radiance of your glory, and I trembled with a combination of love and dread. I seemed to be a long way from you, in a far country, listening to your voice as it spoke to me from above, "I am the food of real men. Grow up and feed on me. But you will never change me into yourself as your digestion changes its food; rather, you will be changed into my likeness."

Then I understood that "thou with rebukes dost correct man for iniquity, thou makest his beauty to consume away like a moth." [8] So I said to myself, "Is truth nothing at all, since it is spatially neither finite nor infinite?" And I heard a voice calling as from afar, "I AM THAT I AM." [9] I heard you as one hears a voice speaking to his heart, and I had no reason whatever to doubt. It would have been easier for me to doubt my existence than to doubt the reality of truth; for it is "clearly seen, being understood by the things that are made." [10]

11

Then I reflected on the orders that are lower than yourself, and saw that they are not altogether real in themselves, yet they are not totally unreal either. They draw their reality from you, and are unreal to the extent that they are not what you are. For only that truly exists which remains unchangeable. So for me it is good to draw near to God and cleave to him; for unless I remain in him, I can't remain in myself. [11] But God, who remains in himself, renews all things. He is my God, and has no need of my goodness. [12]

12

It was shown me that things which undergo corruption are in themselves good. If they were supremely good, of course, they could not be corrupted; but neither could they be corrupted if they were no good in the first place. So either corruption does no harm, which is impossible, or everything that is corrupted is stripped of its good—which is quite certain. But that which is deprived of its good no longer has any being. We conclude that all those things that are divested of goodness cease to exist; but as long as they exist, they are good. Therefore, whatever is, is good; and evil, whose source I had been tracking for so long, is not a substance at all. For if it were a substance, it would be good.

13

For you, Lord, evil has no existence, and not only for you but for your whole created universe, because there is nothing outside creation that can come crashing into it and so disrupt the order you have imposed on it. Yet in parts of your creation there are certain things which are thought to be evil because they don't relate harmoniously to other things. But there are still other things to which they do relate, which makes them good; and in fact they are good in themselves.

14

My soul did not dare to be displeased with my God, and so it would not attribute to you things that it found displeasing in creation. That is why it adopted the theory of two substances [good and evil]. But unknown to me, you stroked my head and closed my eyes so I would not behold vanity,[13] and I slept away some of my crazy ideas. When I woke up in you, I saw that you were infinite, but infinite in a way different from what I had thought; and it was not with the eye of flesh that I reached this conclusion.

15

I looked about at other things and saw that they, too, owe their existence to you: They were all contained by you, not spatially or geographically, but in a unique way. You hold in truth the whole universe in the hollow of your hand, and all things are true insofar as they exist. Falsehood is nothing but the supposed existence of that which never was. I saw, too, that everything that exists agrees not only with its proper place, but with its proper time; because you, who alone are eternal, did not wait until countless ages of time had elapsed before you began to operate. You are the one who makes time come and go, and in fact, without you there is nothing to operate.

16

From my own experience I know it is not surprising when bread that tastes good to a healthy man becomes uninviting to him when he is sick. Light that is pleasant to sound eyes is painful to eyes that are sore. In the same way evildoers find your justice hard to take, harder in fact than the existence of snakes and worms. But snakes and worms you created good. So when I asked what evil was, I found that it was not a substance but a perversion of the will when it becomes bloated with desire for the externals of life and is diverted from you, God, the supreme reality.

17

It seemed strange to me that while I now loved you, rather than some phantasm substituting for you, I did not consistently enjoy my God. Your beauty ravished me, but I was soon snatched away again by the sheer weight of the world and its ways, to collapse dismally in its muck. Yet the memory of you remained with me, and I became convinced there was one to whom I ought to cleave, though I wasn't yet capable of doing it.

By now I was inquiring into an appraisal of earthly and heavenly bodies, and by stages I passed from bodies to the soul, as it operates through the senses, and then to the soul's inner faculty of receiving sense impressions from external objects. That is the limit of animal intelligence. The next stage is the power of reason which judges the facts submitted by the bodily senses. But realizing that this power was subject to change led me to consider the source of its understanding. My mind withdrew from the contradictory fantasies that played upon it, in order to explore the light that bathed it. For without any question the mind cried out that the Unchangeable was superior to the changeable. But how did it know that, unless it knew the Unchangeable? Thus at one trembling flash it arrived at the vision of reality: that which *is*. I saw the invisible nature of God himself.[14]

However, I had not strength to keep looking; in my weakness I recoiled and fell back into my old habits, taking with me nothing but a loving memory, as though I had sniffed the fragrance of eternity but was not able to eat of it.

18

So I looked for a way to obtain the strength I needed to enjoy you, but never found it until I laid hold of that mediator between God and man, the Man Christ Jesus,[15] who is God over all things and blessed forever.[16] He called me and said to me, "I am the way, the truth, and the life." [17] He combined our flesh with the spiritual food I was too weak to eat; for the Word was made flesh [18] in order that your wisdom, by which all things were formed, might be able to provide milk for us who are spiritual infants.

Still I was not humble enough to take the humble Jesus as my God; nor did I know what his taking our weak nature was supposed to teach us. Your Word, the eternal truth, overtops the highest peaks of your creation; and he lifts up those of low degree [19] to himself. Yet he stooped to this human clay of ours and built himself a humble habitation that he might win to himself all who are willing to surrender their own selves. He would heal men of the tumors of their pride. He would nurture their love so they would not become overconfident of their strength, but would recognize their own weakness when they saw before their eyes Divinity himself in his weakness.[20] He shared our coats of skin,[21] so that we would wearily throw ourselves upon his humanity, and so find ourselves lifted up by his resurrection.

19

But I was thinking along other lines. I considered Christ my Lord to be a man of remarkable wisdom whose nativity put him in a class by himself. I took it that his humble birth was a demonstration of the way our loving God holds worldly goods in contempt as compared with the prize of immortality. Christ seemed to me to have great authority as a teacher; but of the mystery of "the Word become flesh" I had not the slightest clue. From what had been handed down to us in Scripture I gathered that Christ ate, drank, slept, walked, talked with people, had his good days and bad days; thus to me any joining of your Word with human flesh meant joining with a human soul and a human mind. Your Word is unchangeable; but as everyone knows, in the properties of a human soul and a human mind there is continual change. Limbs, emotions, speech—all are characterized by motion. If the biblical record did not indicate such things to be true of Christ's life, the whole Bible would be in danger of being branded false, and the human race would no longer find saving faith in it.

Since I considered the Scripture to be true, I conceded that Christ was a complete man: not merely dwelling in a man's body, or having a human soul and body without a human mind, but a man in the full sense of the word. I judged that he was to be preferred over all other men, not because he personified Truth but because of the superb characteristics of his human nature and his access to the fount of wisdom.

20

By reading the books of the Platonists I was taught to look for truth as something immaterial and nonphysical. I saw that the "invisible things" are "understood by the things that are made." [22] And though I was foiled in my ongoing attempt to find the truth, I was able dimly to perceive what the darkness of my mind would not permit me to examine clearly. I became convinced that you existed, and that you were infinite, though not necessarily in spatial terms; and that you were unvarying either in parts or in motion. I was certain that all things derive from you on the strongest possible basis of proof—the fact that they existed.

But as positive as I was about these matters, I was still too puny to enjoy you. I gabbled away as though I were quite the expert, but I had not sought your Way in Christ our Savior, so my "expertise" became my "demise." The reason was that I had now begun to put on a face of wisdom; instead of regretting my condition, I swelled with pride over the new knowledge I had acquired.[23] But where was the love that builds on the foundation of humility in Christ Jesus? And when would these books teach it to me? I believe it was your will that I should come across the Platonists' books before beginning to study your Scriptures, so that I might remember how they affected me. Afterward, when I had been tamed by your texts and my wounds had been touched by your healing fingers, I would be able to discern between presumption and confession; between those who know where they want to go but not how to get there, and those who not only see the way that leads to the land of blessing but who make it there and live in it.

21

So I snatched at the time-honored writings inspired by your Spirit, and especially at the letters of the Apostle Paul. The places in which he seemed to contradict himself and to go against the testimony of Moses and the prophets no longer existed. I looked upon the holy eloquence of your Word as having one face, and like the Psalmist I exulted with trembling.[24] After I began reading, it became clear that whatever truths I had found in the Platonists were contained there also, along with the praise of your Grace. For it is by Grace that a man is taught not only to look upon you, who are forever the same God; but is also given enabling power to take hold of you.

A man may "delight in the law of God in my inmost self," but as Paul says, there is "in my members another law at war with the law of my mind and making me captive to the law of sin which dwells in my members." [25] What shall man do? For you are just, Lord, and we have sinned; we have done wrong and acted wickedly. Your hand is heavy on us. We have been turned over (and justly so) to the ancient power of evil, the prince of death, who has persuaded our wills to become like his will, because he does not stand in your truth.[26] What shall man do in his misery? Who shall deliver him from the body of this death? [27] No one but the Grace of God through Jesus Christ our Lord, who was begotten by you to be co-eternal with you, and was created in the beginning of your way.[28] The prince of this world found nothing in him worthy of death,[29] yet killed him; and the handwriting of the decree against us was thereby wiped out.[30]

None of this is found in the Platonists' books. Their pages fail to reveal the face of devotion, the tears of confession. They never mention that "the sacrifice acceptable to God is a broken spirit; a broken and contrite heart, O God, thou wilt not despise." [31] They are mute on such subjects as the redemption of men, the city prepared as a bride,[32] the pledge of the Holy Spirit,[33] the cup of our salvation.[34] In them no one sings, "Truly my soul waiteth upon God: from him cometh my salvation. He only is my rock and my salvation; he is my defense; I shall not be greatly moved." [35] Nor does anyone hear a voice calling, "Come unto me, all ye that labor." [36] They reject the teaching of him who was meek and lowly of heart; [37] for you have hidden all this from the learned and wise, and have revealed it to the simple.[38]

It is one thing to climb above timber line to the summit and catch a view of the land of peace, then to fail to find a trail leading to it, and so have to struggle through uncharted country, waylaid and beset by fugitives and deserters. It is quite another to move steadily down the posted highway to it, convoyed by the security troops of the King of heaven, unmolested by deserters who avoid the road like the plague. These truths amazingly worked their way into my viscera as I studied the letters of "the least of the apostles," [39] and I looked upon your works and trembled.

BOOK EIGHT

Take Up and Read

1

My God, I want to think back over all your mercies toward me and tell the world about them with a thankful heart. Let my bones be soaked in your love until all my being cries out, "Lord, who is like you? You burst open the chains that bound me. I will offer to you the sacrifice of praise.[1] How you broke my fetters I'm about to tell so that everyone will adore you and say, 'Blessed is the Lord in heaven and on earth; great and marvelous is his name.' " [2]

Your words took root in my heart, and you hemmed me in on every side. I was now certain of your eternal life, though I saw it only as in a glass darkly.[3] I was no longer bothered with doubts about an incorruptible substance from which every other substance takes its being. My aim now was not to become more certain of you, but to become more faithful to you, for in my everyday life I was still wobbling badly. My heart had to be purged of the old leaven.[4] The Way, the Savior himself, charmed me, but I was still unwilling to tread the narrow path. So you put it in my mind, and made it seem a good idea to me to go to see Simplicianus. I considered him to be a good servant of yours, for something of your Grace shone in him.[5] From his youth, I'd heard, he had lived a life of devotion to you. Now he was getting on in years and had gained a great deal of experience. I wanted to talk over my problems with him and learn how a person in my situation could best walk in your Way.

I saw that the church was full of people going this way and that, but I was dissatisfied with the way I was following in the world. The drive for wealth and honors no longer inflamed me, and since my life was now left without hope or ambition, it had become a treadmill. The things of the world no longer delighted me by comparison with your sweetness and the beauty of your house which I loved. But I was still caught in the clutches of sex. The Apostle Paul did not forbid my taking a wife, though he did suggest that there was something better and wished that all men might live as he did.[6] But I was made of weaker stuff, and chose an easier way, and for this reason I was unable to decide about other matters. The whole business exhausted me and kept me in a continuing state of anxiety, for there were many reasons why I was unwilling to face the kind of married life I had promised to enter. I had found the pearl of great price, and I ought to have sold everything to buy it, but I still doubted.

2

So I went to Simplicianus who years before had been given Grace to lead Ambrose to Christ. I knew that Ambrose, who had since become the Bishop of Milan, still loved him as his spiritual father. I told Simplicianus the story of my circuitous wanderings and mentioned that I had read some of the books of the Platonists [7] which Victorinus, the teacher of rhetoric at Rome, had translated into Latin. (Victorinus, so I had heard, afterward died a Christian.) Simplicianus congratulated me on not having been exposed to the writings of other philosophers that were full of misleading fallacies drawn from the "elements of this world." [8] In the Platonists, he felt, God and his Word were implied all the way through.

Then to encourage me toward the humility of Christ which is

hidden from the wise and revealed to children,[9] he told me the story of Victorinus, whom he had known very well when he lived in Rome. I repeat the story here for the praise of the glory of your Grace.[10] Here was an old man, learned and wise, skilled in all the liberal sciences, who had read many philosophical writings and read them with discrimination, the speech instructor of leading senators and one who, as a tribute to his distinguished service, had been voted a statue in the Forum—something the citizens of this world consider an exceptional honor. For years Victorinus had worshiped the traditional idols of Rome and had taken part in the sacrilegious rites that were then popular among the Roman nobility. With thundering eloquence he had defended these practices and yet now, as an old man, he was not embarrassed to be the child of your Christ, submitting his neck to the yoke of humility and bowing his head before the offense of the cross.

O Lord, Lord, who tilted the heavens until they slid, and who touched the mountains and made them smoke,[11] how did you sneak your way into his heart? Victorinus read the Holy Scriptures, Simplicianus told me, and made a thorough investigation of the available Christian literature. Then he said to Simplicianus, not openly but privately as a friend, "You ought to know I am now a Christian." Simplicianus replied, "I'll believe it when I see you in the church of Christ." Victorinus laughed and then asked, "Does simply walking through the hole in a church wall make a man a Christian?"

He often repeated his claim that he was a Christian to his friend, and each time he got the same reply, and Victorinus would then make a joke about the church wall. He was afraid of offending his proud, demon-worshiping friends. However, after more serious study he gathered some inner fortitude, and now he became even more fearful lest Christ should deny him before the holy angels,[12] should he be too timid to confess his Lord before men. So he became brazen toward vanity and sheepish toward the truth, until suddenly and unexpectedly one day he said to Simplicianus, "Let's go to church. I want to be made a Christian." Simplicianus, unable to contain his happiness, went with him.

The time came for Victorinus to make public confession of his faith in Christ. At Rome it was the custom for one giving such a testimony for the first time to mount a platform in the Forum and repeat before the congregation a set form of words committed to memory. The church elders, however, told Victorinus they would make an exception in his case and allow him to give his testimony in private, as they sometimes did with those who were diffident about appearing publicly. But Victorinus preferred to declare his salvation in full view of the holy assembly. He said there had been no saving power in the rhetoric he had taught, yet he had expounded it openly. He had not been afraid to speak his own words before the hostile crowds of Rome. Why should he now hesitate to profess your Word before a gentle flock?

So when he mounted the platform and began to speak, all who knew him (and who didn't?) began nudging each other and whispering in congratulatory tones. A suppressed sound went through the gathered multitude: "Victorinus! Victorinus!" At the sight of him there was an outburst of loud applause; then they quieted down so they could hear him. He pronounced with clear confidence his belief in the true faith, and everyone wanted to reach out and take him into their hearts. And that, in fact, is just what they did.

3

Good God, what affects men that they should get more excited over the salvation of a soul everyone had given up for lost, or one narrowly delivered from danger, than over a soul that was never beyond either hope or rescue? You, too, merciful Father, rejoice more "over one sinner who repents than over ninety-nine righteous persons who need no repentance." [13] We shout for joy to hear that the shepherd has brought back on his shoulders the sheep that strayed, and that the lost drachma is returned to your treasury while the neighbors celebrate with the woman who found it. The happy festivities in your home bring tears to our eyes as we listen to the story of how your younger son was dead and came to life, was lost and found again. It is a fact of experience that the greater the happiness, the greater the trouble that preceded it. But why is this, Lord my God, when you are eternal, when you are joy itself, and are surrounded by those who are always delighting in you? It's too much for me! You're too high in the heights and too deep in the depths. You never leave us, but it's hard to come back to you.

5

When your man Simplicianus told me this story about Victorinus, I burned to imitate him—which of course is why Simplicianus had related it. He also said that in the reign of the emperor Julian [14] a decree was issued prohibiting Christians from teaching literature and oratory, and Victorinus obeyed the law by giving up his school of rhetoric rather than forsaking your Word which makes even a child eloquent. In doing so Victorinus, as I viewed it, was making not so much a show of bravery as a happy choice, for it enabled him to devote himself wholly to you. That's what I too was pining for, but I was bound—not by somebody else's irons but by my own iron will. The enemy had taken hold of my will; he had clamped a chain on it and shackled it. For my will had been perverted and had manufactured lust; the more I gave in to lust, the more it developed into a habit, and when I failed to check the habit it became a necessity. These were all links in the chain that held me enslaved. The new will that had begun in me—and made me want to be free to worship and to enjoy you, God, the only certain joy—was not yet strong enough to overpower the old will that had become tough with age. So there were now two wills battling it out inside me, one old, one new; one carnal, one spiritual; and in the conflict they ripped my soul to pieces.

From my own experience I know, therefore, what Paul meant when he said, "The flesh lusts against the Spirit, and the Spirit against the flesh." [15] I was on both sides, but mostly I was on the side that I approved in myself, rather than the side I disapproved. When I did things that I knew were wrong I did not act willingly, but just endured them; but habit had been reinforced by that part of my will that had deserted to the enemy, so it was by my own will that I found myself in a spot I didn't want to be in. And what point is there in complaining when a sinner gets what is coming to him? I used to excuse myself by saying I had no clear concept of truth, and that was why I still followed the ways of the world rather than serve you. Now, however, I was quite certain about the truth; and still I kept myself grounded and refused to enlist in your service. I was more afraid of getting rid of my frustrations than I was of being frustrated.

Thus I was put under pressure by the oppressions of the world, but I took it all with a light heart, like a man sound asleep. When I did think about you, my meditations were like the feeble struggles of a man who is trying to wake up but is overcome with drowsiness and falls back to sleep. I had no answer when you said, "Awake, O sleeper, and arise from the dead, and Christ shall give you light." [16] You used every possible means to communicate to me the truth of your words. You had me under conviction so that I could give no reply except a lazy and drowsy, "Yes, Lord, yes, I'll get to it right away, just don't bother me for a little while." But "right away" didn't happen right away; and "a little while" turned out to be a very long while. In my inmost self I delighted in the law of God, but I perceived that there was in my bodily members a different law fighting against the law that my reason approved and making me a prisoner under the law that was in my members, the law of sin.[17] For the law of sin is the force of habit, by which the mind is carried along and held prisoner against its will, deservedly, of course, because it slid into the habit by its own choice. Messed-up creature that I was, who was there to rescue this doomed body? God alone, through Jesus Christ our Lord! [18]

6

How you delivered me of the desire for sensual pleasure that held me chained, and from the tyranny of the things of this world, I will now describe and give praise to your name, O Lord, my strength and my redeemer.[19] As I went about my usual tasks I became increasingly uneasy, and this was reflected in my daily prayers to you. I went to church whenever I had leisure from my work, which had become an increasing drag on me.

Alypius was staying with me, having been released from his legal post after a third term as assessor. One day when Nebridius was absent (for a reason I can't recall) a man named Ponticianus came to visit us. He was a fellow countryman from Africa who held a high position in the imperial palace. I haven't any idea what he came to see us about, but when we sat down to talk, he noticed a book lying on a game table in front of us. He picked it up, opened it, and found to his astonishment that it contained the letters of the Apostle Paul. My friend had imagined it would be one or another of my textbooks on rhetoric that wore me out as a teacher. He studied me intently, then smiled and expressed his surprise and delight at discovering this book—and only this book—there before me.

Ponticianus was a solid Christian who would often be found in church kneeling before you, our God, and praying at some length. When I indicated that I was giving considerable attention to the Scriptures, a discussion rose among us about the Egyptian monk Anthony,[20] whose name was held in high regard among your servants, although until Ponticianus told Alypius and me about him we had never even heard of him. When our African friend discovered our ignorance, which was hard for him to believe, he proceeded to fill us in with some detail. We were surprised, too, to hear a testimony of your mighty works performed so recently as to be practically in our own time, within the life and fellowship of the believing church. So we all wondered—we, to hear that such great things had taken place, and he, that we had never heard of them.

As Ponticianus continued to chat with us, he told about going for an afternoon walk with three companions during a visit to Trier,[21] where the emperor was taking in the chariot races at the circus. It seems the route the four strollers took led to some gardens near the city wall, where they divided into pairs, Ponticianus accompanying one friend while the other two went off by themselves. The latter pair apparently wandered aimlessly until they came to a little cottage where some servants of yours live who are poor in spirit but rich in the Kingdom of heaven. There the visitors found a book containing the life of Anthony. One of them began reading it and became so fired up and gripped by it that before he finished, he began to consider the possibility of taking up such a life as Anthony's and leaving his government career to serve you. Both men, it seems, were members of the imperial secret police.

The one who had been reading about Anthony was filled with a love of holiness and a corresponding sense of shame and anger at himself. He fixed his eyes on his friend and said, "Look, what is all this energy we're expending doing for us? Do you have any idea? What do we expect to achieve in government service? Anything higher than 'friends of the emperor'? So what's that? A flimsy and risky proposition at best if you ask me. It means landing in one hot spot after another, and each one more dangerous. Who knows whether we'll ever make it to the top? But if I want to, I can become a friend of God right this minute!"

As the man finished speaking, it was evident to those listening that he was in the throes of the new life generating within him. He turned back to the book and continued to read. The interior change taking place was one that you alone could see, for his mind was starting to put aside the world and its ways. As he went on reading his heart seemed to be turning over, and at one point he cried out involuntarily as he made his decision for a different kind of life. As he was now yours, he told his friend, "I have dropped all my old ambitions and hopes and have decided to serve God, beginning here and now in this place. You may not want to imitate me, but please don't get in my way." His friend replied that he would stick with him so that together they would share the rewards of such a life. Both men now being yours, they set about building a tower after counting the cost,[22] which meant giving up everything they had to follow you.

7

That was the substance of what Ponticianus told us. While he was still speaking, Lord, you were turning me around toward myself, taking me from behind my own back where I had hid myself so I would not have to look at me. You set me before my own face so I could see how rotten I was, how warped, cheap, and shabby. I saw it all and became disgusted because there was no way I could run away from myself. If I tried to divert my thinking to something else, there was Ponticianus sitting there going on and on with his story. You used him to force me back once more to confront the sin that I loathed. I had known about my sin all right, but had been in the habit either of overlooking it, or pretending it wasn't there, or forgetting it.

But my heart warmed up to those two men as I heard of the saving change that had taken place in them, and the way they had surrendered themselves completely to you and had been made whole. When I compared myself to them it made me curse myself in a fit of revulsion. Many years had gone downstream (twelve, I believe) since my nineteenth year when I had first read Cicero's *Hortensius* and had been inspired to devote my life to the study of wisdom and philosophy. Yet here I was, still putting off the rejection of this world and its pleasures which would have freed me to take up such an investigation. I know now that not only the finding of wisdom, but even the seeking of it, tips the scales on balance against all the kingdoms and treasures of this world and all the voluptuous delights the human body has to offer. But as an adolescent I had prayed a pitiful prayer for a clean life, saying, "Give me chastity and give me control over myself, *but not yet.*" I was afraid you might answer me too quickly and straighten me out before I was ready; for what I really wanted was not to be cured but to be fulfilled.

I felt the reason I had stalled from day to day, and refused to give up the hope of this world in order to follow you only, was because it was unclear to me what course I should pursue. Now the time came when I stood stripped naked before myself, and my conscience chided me: "Where are you, tongue? Didn't you say you would never throw off your load of vanity as long as the truth was uncertain? Well, here is your certainty; now why are you still toting it around? Here are others who have freed their shoulders and received wings instead, and they didn't have to wear themselves out for ten years scarching out truth and trying to make up their minds." So this thing kept gnawing at me all the time Ponticianus was speaking, and I was flung into shame and confusion. He brought his story to a close, wound up the purpose of his visit and went away, leaving me to deal with myself. And what didn't I have to say? How I beat myself with words, and tried to lash my soul into following me as I endeavored to follow you! But it fought back. It refused to obey, yet offered no excuse. By now every argument had been worn threadbare and exposed, but my soul remained fearful and silent. What really bothered it was giving up the habits that were killing it.

8

A first-class uproar now broke out in the house of my inner self, as I began brawling with my soul in our common meeting place— my heart. Agitated in mind and expression, I turned upon Alypius and cried, "What's the matter with us? What is this we've been hearing? These half-learned men rise up and seize heaven by force,[23] and we pusillanimous cowards, with all our education, lie here wallowing in our flesh and blood. Are we ashamed to follow just because someone else has led the way? Isn't it a greater shame not to follow at all?"

I don't know what I said really, but it was something like that. My emotional excitement caused me to break away from Alypius while he gaped at me thunderstruck. I couldn't talk in a normal voice. My forehead, cheeks, eyes, color, and tone of voice all spoke of what was going on in my mind more eloquently than the words I used. There was a small garden adjoining the quarters where we stayed, and we had the use of it as well as of the whole house while the owner was away. To this spot the commotion in my heart drove me.

Here, it seemed, no one could interrupt the heated quarrel I was pressing against myself until it should resolve itself in some way I didn't know—but you did. I was out of my mind with a severe malady that would bring health to my soul. I was dying to the world that I might live for you. The evil in me I knew all about, but the good that was soon to come I wasn't familiar with. So I slipped into the garden with Alypius at my heels, for what secret did I have that he didn't know about? And how could he have deserted me in such a state of mind? We sat down as far as we could from the house. My spirit was roaring in indignation because I had not entered into an agreement and pact with you, my God. It was something for which all my bones cried out, praising the idea to the skies. But this is not something men sail into aboard their ships, or ride into in their chariots, or walk into on their feet, even the little distance from the house to where we were sitting. To set out and to arrive there, nothing more is required than the will to get going. But it had to be a resolute will, and a single-minded will, not something half-crippled and divided, not a will that twisted and tossed and wrestled with itself, with one part moving ahead and the other part sagging and collapsing.

In the emotional excitement created by my hesitation, I engaged in various random actions. I tugged at my hair and pounded my forehead and locked my fingers and hugged my knees, each bit of behavior resulting from a specific act of will. But to will is not always the same as to be able. I might have willed these things and still not have done them—as would be the case if my limbs had been unable to respond. And what I longed to do above everything else, I now found impossible. Had I brought a single-minded will to the problem, I could have done it at once, for in that case the will to do it and the power to act would be the same thing. When my mind tried to force itself to will the one thing it wanted most to do, it floundered.

9

Why does this monstrosity occur? The mind gives an order to the body and it is obeyed on the spot; it gives an order to itself and is rebuffed. It won't carry out its own command! The reason is that it does not fully will to do it. There are actually two wills in us, and neither one is the whole will by itself.

10

When I vacillated about my decision to serve the Lord my God, it was I who willed and I who willed not, and nobody else. I was fighting against myself. As the Apostle would say, "It was no longer I that was doing it, but sin which dwells within me." [24] Such was the penalty of a sin committed in conditions of greater freedom by Adam, whose son I am.

11

And such was my psychological condition. I kept condemning myself bitterly while twisting and turning in my chains, trying to break them, because it was a very small matter that still held me.

Yet hold me it did; and in the secret recess of my heart, Lord, you never let up the pressure. I kept saying to myself, "Now! Now!" and had myself just about talked into it; but not quite. I took a deep breath and tried again, and each time came a little closer, and a little closer, so I could almost reach out and take hold of it. But I couldn't hold it or even touch it, because I hesitated to take the step that would make me die to death and live to life. I was too accustomed to the worst in me and too unaccustomed to the better. The closer it got to the time when I was to become something else, the more terror it aroused in me. But the approaching what-ever-it-was didn't hit back or turn me off, it just kept me in suspense.

I was held back by trifling nonsense—old loves that plucked softly at my robe of flesh and murmured, "Are you going to send us away? From this moment, forever and ever? It means you will never be allowed to do this and that again." And what were they suggesting by what I call "this and that"? My God, let your mercy keep the soul of your servant from such actions! Now I could only half hear these voices, for they were not openly contradicting me by opposing me face to face, but were muttering behind my back and secretly tugging at my sleeve, trying to get me to turn around and look their way. And they did manage to slow me down, so that I hesitated to tear myself away and shake them off and leap across to where I was called to be. The pull of habit was still too much for me when it asked, "Do you think you can live without these things?" This controversy in my heart was entirely between me and myself; meanwhile Alypius stayed at my side, silently awaiting the outcome of this strange emotional crisis.

12

My introspection plumbed the secret depths and brought to-gether all my misery in plain sight of my heart, so that a great storm broke, bringing a shower of tears. In order to pour out the whole tempest without holding back, I got up and walked away from Alypius, as it seemed to me that solitude was the best climate for the business of crying. I went to a corner of the garden where I wouldn't be bothered by his presence. He sensed what my feelings were, for I probably said something in which the choking in my voice told that I was on the verge of tears. So I left, and he sat there more dumfounded than ever.

In some way, I'm not just sure how, I threw myself down under a fig tree and let the tears gush freely. These were the streams that proved a sacrifice acceptable to you, my Lord. Not in the exact words of Scripture but in some similar vein I talked with you for a long time. I asked, "And thou, Lord, how long wilt thou be roused to such fury? Do not remember the sins of former times" [25]—for I felt they were still holding me. I ended on a dismal note: "How long, how long? Tomorrow and tomorrow? Why not now? Why not put an end to my sin right this hour?"

I was going on like this, weeping in bitter dejection of spirit, when I heard a voice coming from the house next door. Whether it was a boy's or a girl's I don't know, but it was singing over and over in a kind of chant, "Take up and read, take up and read." Immediately my demeanor changed. I thought back over the children's games I knew, trying to recall whether I had ever heard such an expression used. I knew of no such game. Stanching the flow of tears, I stood up, for I could only interpret the words as a kind of divine command to open the Scripture [26] and read the first passage I came across. I had heard how Anthony once dropped in unexpectedly at a church service during a reading of the gospel, and was inspired by what he heard as if it were addressed to him personally: "Go and sell what you have and give it to the poor, and you shall have treasure in heaven; and come and follow me." [27] By this word from the Lord he was converted to you right on the spot. So I returned quickly to the bench where Alypius was sitting. When I had moved from there I'd left behind the copy of the letters of the Apostle. Now I grabbed up the book, opened it, and read silently the first portion of Scripture on which my eyes lighted: "Not in reveling and drunkenness, not in debauchery and licentiousness, not in quarreling and jealousy. But put on the Lord Jesus Christ, and make no provision for the flesh, to gratify its desires." [28] I had no need or wish to read further, for when I came to the end of the sentence, instantly, it seemed, a light of certainty turned on in my heart and all the fog of doubt disappeared.

Then marking the place by inserting my finger between the pages or in some way or other, I shut the book and in a tranquil frame of mind told Alypius what had happened. He confided something of what had been occupying his own thoughts—which I knew nothing about. He asked to see what I had just been reading and I showed him. He then looked beyond the passage. I had no idea what followed, but it was this: "As for the man who is weak in faith, welcome him." [29] Alypius told me he applied those words to himself. They provided motive power to strengthen his determination to resolve his own situation and—without stalling and without making waves—to join me in a good purpose. It was just like him to do it, for his moral character had been better than mine for a long, long time.

We went into the house and gave my mother the news and she was overjoyed. When we explained to her how it had all come about, she was exuberant and triumphant and gave thanks to you who are "able to do far more abundantly than all that we ask or think." [30] She saw that you had given her, on my behalf, far more than she was used to asking for in all her sobbings and groanings and wailings. You had converted me to yourself on the same rule of faith you had revealed to her so many years before,[31] and had turned all her mourning into gladness.[32]

BOOK NINE

Genius Afire

1

Who am I? What am I like? Of what evil am I not capable, in either deed or word or will? But you are good and merciful, Lord. Your right hand reached to the bottom of my heart and emptied out its dregs of death and corruption. All you asked was that I cease to want what I willed, and begin to want what you willed. But where had my free will been hiding during all those years? From what secret cranny did you summon it at a moment's notice, so I might bend my neck to your easy yoke and my shoulders to your light burden, Christ Jesus, my strength and my redeemer? [1] How good it felt to be done with the delectable trifles of life! Those things I had been afraid to let go, it now became a joy to dispense with. You drove them away from me, you who are the true and highest joy. You drove them away and came in yourself with a sweetness beyond all pleasure (though not to flesh and blood), brighter than every light (though the most hidden of all lights), and higher than every honor (but not to those who build up their own). My mind was free at last from the corroding anxiety of running around trying to get somewhere, and continually scratching the itch of lust. I talked to you freely as a child talks to its father, Lord my God, my light, my treasure, and my salvation.

4

As I began to read the Psalms of David, those hymns of faith and devotion that break the pompous spirit, they made me literally cry out to you, my God. I was a raw beginner, new to your love, and now the Psalms were setting me on fire and making me want to shout them to the whole world, to counteract the pride of the human race. The truth is, of course, that they *are* sung throughout the world, and none can escape your burning heat.[2] When your Spirit spoke to us through the Psalmist, "Mortal men, how long will you pay me not honor but dishonor, or set your heart on trifles and run after lies?" [3] I alternately shuddered with fear and waxed warm in the hope that exults in your mercy, Father. It showed in my eyes and could be heard in my voice, for I had done just that: set my heart on trifles and run after lies.

But you, Lord, had already magnified your Holy One. You raised him from the dead and seated him at your right hand,[4] where he kept his promise by sending to us the Paraclete, the Spirit of Truth. He sent the Holy Spirit and I didn't even know it! So the Prophet cries out in the Fourth Psalm, "How long?" and he warns, "Hear this!" and when I heard those words I trembled, for I remembered that I was just the kind of person he was talking about. The phantasms I once believed in were trifles and lies. No wonder I cried out in sorrow over the past! I wish some of those today who love trifles and lies could have heard me. Perhaps they would be disturbed enough to repent of their mistakes. I know this: If they did, you would listen to them when they called upon you. For when Christ died in the flesh, he truly died for us, and he lives today before you to make intercession for us.

6

In due time we were baptized, and all anxiety over the past life fled from us. I never tired in those days of thinking about the wonders of your love and the profundity of your plan of salvation for the human race. When I listened to your hymns and songs it made me weep, for I was cut to the quick by the melodies of the singing church. As its voices flowed into my ear, and the truth was distilled into my heart, my feelings of devotion bubbled over and the tears ran down. I was happy.

BOOK TEN

What Is My God?

1

Let me know you, my Knower. Let me know you even as you know me.[1] Power of my soul, enter into it and make it fit for yourself, without spot or wrinkle, then claim it and possess it.[2] That's what I hope for, and why I speak out. That hope is what really gives me the joy of my salvation. As for the other things in life—the more we moan about them, the less they deserve our attention. For you delight in the truth, and he who practices the truth comes to the light.[3] And my heart's desire in making this confession is to set forth the truth, first in your presence, and then by means of this writing before many witnesses.

2

And so, my God, my confession is made to you both silently and audibly. For even if I make no sound in your presence, my inaudible emotions are making plenty of noise! Whatever I say to men that is right was first said to you privately; and whatever it was I said to you, you said it to me first.

3

What difference does it make to me whether men hear my confession or not—as if they could cure all my ailments! Men are an inquisitive lot, curious to find out about other people's lives, lazy when it comes to doing anything about their own. Why do they want to hear from me what I'm like, when they won't listen to you, Lord, when you tell them what they're like? How do they know whether what they hear from me or about me is the truth, since no one knows "a man's thoughts, except the man's own spirit that is within him"? [4]

But when they hear about themselves from you they cannot say, "The Lord lies." For to hear about themselves from you is to see themselves as they really are. And when a man sees that, he can't say, "That is false," without becoming a liar himself. So, because love believes all things [5]—among those who are bound together by love—I will make my confession to you in order that men might hear. I can't prove to them that I am confessing the truth, but those whose ears have been opened to me by love will believe me.

Please, Physician of my inner life, make clear to me what fruit will result from this speaking out. I know you have forgiven my past sins, and have drawn a tapestry over them, to give me happiness in yourself and to transform my life by faith and baptism. And others read or hear of what has happened to me and their hearts get excited. They come out of their listlessness or desperation in which they think, "It's too much to expect God to notice me," and wake up to the love of your mercy and the delights of your Grace. Then they realize that the man who is weak is made strong when he becomes conscious of his weakness. [6] But the good people are happy to hear of the past sins of people who are rid of them, not because they are pleased to hear about evil, but they're so glad it's over and done with.

6

I love you, Lord, not doubtingly, but with absolute certainty. Your Word beat upon my heart until I fell in love with you, and now the universe and everything in it tells me to love you, and tells the same thing to us all, so that we are without excuse.[7]

And what do I love when I love you? Not physical beauty, or the grandeur of our existence in time, or the radiance of light that pleases the eye, or the sweet melody of old familiar songs, or the fragrance of flowers and ointments and spices, or the taste of manna or honey, or the arms we like to use to clasp each other. None of these do I love when I love my God. Yet there is a kind of light, and a kind of melody, and a kind of fragrance, and a kind of food, and a kind of embracing, when I love my God. They are the kind of light and sound and odor and food and love that affect the senses of my inner man. There is another dimension of life in which my soul reflects a light that space itself cannot contain. It hears melodies that never fade with time. It inhales lovely scents that are not blown away by the wind. It eats without diminishing or consuming the supply. It never gets separated from the embrace of God and never gets tired of it. That is what I love when I love my God.

And what is my God? I asked the earth and it replied, "I am not he"; and everything in it said the same thing. I asked the sea, the abyss of the deep, and the crawling things that live in it, and they answered, "We are not your God. Look above us." I asked the gentle breezes, and the air and everything in the atmosphere responded, "Anaximenes * was wrong. I am not God." I asked the heavens, the sun, the moon and stars. They said to me, "Neither

---

* Anaximenes of Miletus was a Greek philosopher of the sixth century B.C. who held that air is the primary substance and that all things are derived from it.

are we the God you seek." I said to all those sensory objects that cluster around my body and cause it to react, "You speak of God and say you are not he. Then tell me something about him." And they all cried out with a loud voice, "He made us!" I questioned them by fixing my attention on them, and their beauty was their answer.

Then I turned to myself and said, "Who are you?" And I replied, "A man." But in me are present both body and soul, one exterior, the other interior. Which should I impress to help me find my God? With my physical apparatus I had already searched for him from earth to sky, as far as my eye could see. But the interior equipment is better. The messengers of my body delivered to it the answers of heaven and earth and everything in them when they told me, "We are not God," and, "He made us." The inner man knows these things by means of the ministering of the outer man. The inner "I" knows them; I, the soul, know them through the senses of the body. So I asked the whole frame of the universe about my God and it answered me back, "I am not he, but he made me."

27

I came to love you late, O Beauty so ancient and so new; I came to love you late. You were within me and I was outside, where I rushed about wildly searching for you like some monster loose in your beautiful world. You were with me but I was not with you. You called me, you shouted to me, you broke past my deafness. You bathed me in your light, you wrapped me in your splendor, you sent my blindness reeling. You gave out such a delightful fragrance, and I drew it in and came breathing hard after you. I tasted, and it made me hunger and thirst; you touched me, and I burned to know your peace.

29

All my hopes are in your great mercy and nowhere else. So give what you command, and command what you will. It is your order that we should practice self-control; the man who insists on loving something besides you does not really love you as he should, unless he loves it because of you. O Love that always burns and is never extinguished! O Love that is my God, set me afire!

42

From what I hear, many who have tried unsuccessfully to find you in their own strength have been led on to experiment with different superstitious practices. As a result they have fallen into a predilection for curious visions and have got what they deserved: delusion. They were probably inflated by their pride of learning and so were misled into seeking you by throwing out their chests rather than beating upon their breasts. So they drew to themselves as partners and allies of their pride, by a kind of inner affinity, the sinister powers of the air.[8] In other words, they sought a mediator between themselves and you by whom they could be made clean through the influence of magic; but they found none. The devil, of course, transformed himself into an angel of light.[9] The very fact that the devil was without a body proved a strong attraction for the pride of men very much aware of their bodies.

But you, Lord, to whom men want to be reconciled, are yourself immortal and sinless. A true mediator between God and man ought to have something in common with God and something in common with men. But that false mediator by whom you, in your hidden counsels, allow human pride to be hoodwinked, does have one thing in common with man: namely, sin. And he would like to think that he also has something in common with God: immortality. It is true he is not covered with mortal flesh; but since the wages of sin are death,[10] the devil suffers this fate in common with man and stands under the same condemnation.

43

The truth is, there is one mediator whom you in your hidden mercy have revealed to the meek and lowly, and have sent as an example of humility to be followed. That is the mediator between God and man, the Man Christ Jesus,[11] who has appeared between mortal sinners and the immortal Just One. As men are, he was mortal; as God is, he was just. And because righteousness issues in life and peace, he, through his righteousness with God, nullified the death of justified sinners by sharing their lot with them. He was revealed to holy men in the past so that they might find salvation through faith in his coming passion, just as we are saved through faith in what his passion has done for us. Insofar as he was man, he is a true mediator; but insofar as he was the Word of God, he is in no intermediary position, for he is equal with God, he is God with God, and together one God.

How much you loved us, Good Father, who spared not your own Son but gave him up for us sinners! [12] How much you loved us, since it was on our behalf that he, who thought it no robbery to be equal with you, submitted himself to the death of the cross.[13] He alone was free among the dead [14] because he was free to lay down his life and free to take it again.[15] For us he was both victor and victim, or should I say, victor because victim. In other words, he became our priest and sacrifice to you, and so the sacrifice became the priest.[16] By being born your Son, and then becoming a slave to serve us, he made us to become your sons. So I have good reason for my strong hope in him who sits at your right hand and makes intercession for us. If I didn't have that hope I would be desperate.

But I believe that in him you will heal all my weaknesses, and they are many and great, many and great; but your medicine is even greater. It would be easy to think that your Word is too remote for any communication with man. It would be easy to despair, had not the Word become flesh to dwell in our midst.[17]

In terror of my sins, and with a millstone of misery hanging around my neck, I began thinking (and my heart began agitating) about taking flight into the solitude of the desert. But you put a halt to that and confirmed your way to me, telling me that since Christ died for all men, those who live should no longer live to themselves, but to him who died for all.[18] So, Lord, I am casting all my cares on you,[19] so that I may live and "consider wondrous things" out of your law.[20] You know my weakness and my ignorance; teach me and make me whole. Your only Son, in whom are hid all the treasures of wisdom and knowledge,[21] has redeemed me with his blood. Don't let proud men heap calumny on me. I think all the time about the cost of that ransom; and not only do I keep thinking about it, but I eat and drink and communicate it. As a beggar, I yearn to be filled by him in the midst of those who eat and are satisfied.[22] For as the Psalmist promised, those who seek the Lord shall praise him.[23]

Notes

BOOK ONE · *Infancy and Childhood*

1. Psalm 145:3.
2. Psalm 147:5.
3. Cf. James 4:6, KJV.
4. This is one of the more widely known quotations from Augustine's *Confessions*.
5. Romans 10:14, RSV.
6. Psalm 22:26, RSV.
7. Psalm 139:8, KJV.
8. Jeremiah 23:24, RSV.
9. Psalm 18:31, RSV.
10. Cf. Psalm 35:3.
11. Psalm 19:12-13, RSV.
12. Psalm 116:10.
13. Psalm 32:5.
14. Psalm 130:3.
15. Psalm 42:11; 43:5, KJV.
16. Gibb calls this passage "a characteristically accurate piece of minute psychological observation" (*Confessions of Augustine*, [London: Cambridge University Press, 1927], p. 8).

17. Psalm 102:27.
18. *Ibid.*
19. However, Scripture does not say (nor does Augustine) that infants are accountable for their sins. Cf. Mark 10:14.
20. Psalm 92:1.
21. Psalm 51:5.
22. The whipping might have been a cane applied to the hands or a rod to the body (Gibb, *op. cit.*, p. 14).
23. Psalm 94:22.
24. Augustine speaks of the church as the spiritual home of all believers in Christ.
25. Infant baptism was not established in general use among the churches until the fifth century. Many followers of Christ in Augustine's day (like Emperor Constantine and Augustine's own father, Patricius) deferred baptism until the hour of death, thinking of it as a sacrament not of initiation but of fulfillment. Salt, on the other hand, was placed on the tongue of a catechumen in North Africa at stated times (cf. Gibb, *op. cit.*, pp. 17-18).
26. Psalm 78:39, KJV.
27. Citations from Vergil's *Aeneid* on this and succeeding pages are taken from Book 1, 38; Book 2, 772; Book 6, 457.
28. Psalm 73:27.
29. Cf. Psalm 40:15.
30. James 4:4.
31. Psalm 86:15.
32. Cf. Psalm 27:8.
33. Luke 15:11-24.
34. The grammatical slip will be recognized more quickly in Britain than in America. Apparently an unlettered North African treated the Latin aspirant (as in *homo*) much as the British Cockney treats it in his own tongue. Augustine's point is well taken.
35. Psalm 123:1, KJV.
36. Matthew 18:3.

BOOK TWO · *The Pears of Adolescence*

1. Psalm 39:11.
2. 1 Corinthians 7:28; 7:1; 7:32-33; translator's rendition.
3. Matthew 19:12.
4. Psalm 116:16.
5. Jeremiah 50:8; 51:6.
6. The reference is to chastity such as Augustine later embraced.
7. Psalm 73:7.
8. Psalm 64:10, KJV.
9. Lucius Sergius Catilina (108-62 B.C.) was a Roman army officer who entered into conspiracy to assassinate the governing consuls and plunder Rome. He is described as being "of great physical strength, reckless, ambitious, unscrupulous, with a certain charm which blinded many to his true nature" (*Oxford Classical Dictionary*). The conspiracy was broken up by Cicero.
10. Cicero, *In Catilinam*, 1-4.
11. Psalm 116:12.
12. Romans 6:21.
13. Psalm 19:12, KJV.
14. Matthew 25:21.

BOOK THREE · *The Young Carthaginian*

1. 2 Corinthians 2:16, KJV.
2. In context it would appear that Augustine is speaking metaphorically in this passage.
3. Deuteronomy 32:17.
4. Romans 7:5.
5. Cicero's treatise *Hortensius* has been lost in antiquity, but it consisted of two books in praise of the study of philosophy. Fragments are quoted in Augustine's writings.

6. Job 12:13, KJV.
7. Colossians 2:8-9, RSV.
8. ᴌ John 2:4.
9. The sun and moon played important roles in the Manichean system, being considered in a certain sense divine.
10. Luke 15:16.
11. Cf. Genesis 3:8; 18:33.
12. Augustine's reference tells us something about the customs of a Roman household. Servants were assigned particular duties and were forbidden others.
13. For offenses against nature, Augustine uses the term *flagitia*; for crimes against society, *facinora*. He continues to contrast the two types of behavior in Section 9 and in Book 4, Section 15.
14. 1 John 2:16.
15. Acts 26:14.
16. Psalm 78:38.
17. Psalm 102:20.
18. Cf. Genesis 22:1-2.
19. Cf. Psalm 144:7.
20. Psalm 86:13.
21. The measuring rule was the "rule of faith," that is, the gospel of Jesus Christ.
22. Cf. Psalm 10:17.
23. Psalm 69:2.
24. Psalm 88:2.
25. The bishop's name remains unknown.

BOOK FOUR • *The Rhetor as Dilettante*

1. 2 Timothy 3:13, KJV.
2. The liberal arts taught by Augustine included rhetoric, grammar, literature, philosophy, mathematics, and music.
3. Psalm 106:47.

4. Psalm 50:14, RSV.
5. Psalm 74:21, KJV.
6. Psalm 4:2.
7. Psalm 73:27.
8. Hosea 12:1.
9. In Augustine's day the Latin term *mathematicus,* like the Greek term *astrologos,* had degenerated in popular usage.
10. Cf. Psalm 41:4.
11. Cf. John 5:14.
12. Matthew 16:27; Romans 2:6; Psalm 51:17.
13. His name was Vindicianus, as Augustine later indicates.
14. James 4:6; 1 Peter 5:5.
15. Augustine was not, of course, acquainted with modern psychological theories of the unconscious, but this rendering seems to be close to the meaning of the Latin.
16. Romans 5:5, RSV.
17. Cf. Psalm 106:2.
18. Cf. Romans 11:33.
19. Psalm 43:5, RSV.
20. Psalm 43:5, KJV.
21. The story is told in Ovid, *Tristia,* IV, 4:74.
22. Psalm 25:15, RSV.
23. Horace, of Vergil, Ode I, 3:8.
24. He is referring to the Manichean religious teaching.
25. Jeremiah 23:24.
26. Psalm 80:7, KJV.
27. John 1:4.
28. Psalm 19:5.
29. John 1:10, KJV.
30. 1 Timothy 1:15.
31. Psalm 41:4.
32. Psalm 73:9.
33. Matthew 10:30.
34. Ephesians 4:14, KJV.

35. Psalm 72:18, KJV.
36. Cf. 1 Corinthians 8:6, KJV.
37. Psalm 18:28, KJV.
38. John 1:16, KJV.
39. John 1:9, KJV.
40. James 1:17, KJV.
41. Cf. 1 Peter 5:5, KJV.
42. Psalm 78:39, KJV.
43. Augustine refers to Christians of his acquaintance in Carthage.
44. John 3:29, NEB.
45. Psalm 51:8, RSV.
46. *Ibid.*
47. The first part of Aristotle's *Organon.*
48. Cf. Genesis 3:18-19.
49. Luke 15:13.
50. The Christians of Augustine's acquaintance.
51. Cf. Psalm 17:8.

BOOK FIVE · *A Barque to Italy*

1. Cf. Psalm 35:10.
2. Psalm 19:6, KJV.
3. Revelation 7:17.
4. Psalm 147:5.
5. 1 Corinthians 1:30, RSV.
6. Isaiah 53:12.
7. Matthew 17:27; 22:21.
8. This entire passage is based on Romans 1:21-25; in our translation the RSV has been followed.
9. Psalm 18:5.
10. Psalm 37:23, NEB.
11. Psalm 142:5, KJV.
12. Psalm 41:4, KJV.

13. The Platonic Academy of skeptics, established in Athens in the third century B.C., taught the necessity of suspended judgment in all questions of truth.

14. If Augustine had been a Christian, he probably would not have been awarded the post, as Symmachus, a distinguished orator himself, was a leader of the pagan opposition to Christianity.

15. Psalm 4:7; 45:7; Ephesians 5:18.

16. Psalm 119:155.

BOOK SIX · *Locked in Immortal Combat*

1. Job 35:11.
2. John 4:14, KJV.
3. 2 Timothy 2:15.
4. Genesis 1:27, RSV.
5. The Roman emperor was Valentinian II, at that time fifteen or sixteen years old.
6. He is referring to the intellectual awakening he experienced on reading Cicero's essay *Hortensius*. See p. 38.
7. 1 Peter 5:7.
8. According to the best information available, in the Roman Empire the normal minimum legal age for marriage was twelve years.
9. Adeodatus ("gift of God"), the brilliant child of Augustine and his mistress of eleven years, was born in Africa in 372. He died about 390, a year before Augustine was ordained.
10. Alypius, Augustine's closest friend and onetime pupil, was also born in Thagaste. He followed Augustine into the Manichean religion, and later received baptism with him from Ambrose. About A.D. 394 Alypius was named Bishop of Thagaste. Nebridius, also an African, was converted from Manicheism shortly after Augustine and Alypius.
11. Epicurus (342?-270 B.C.) was a Greek philosopher who taught that pleasure is the only good in life and the goal of all morality.

BOOK SEVEN · *The Anatomy of Evil*

1. Psalm 38:8, KJV.
2. Psalm 103:9.
3. James 4:6, RSV.
4. The preceding quotations, principally from RSV, are cited from John 1:1-14.
5. Philippians 2:6-8.
6. Cf. Matthew 11:29, KJV.
7. Psalm 30:10.
8. Psalm 39:11, KJV.
9. Exodus 3:14, KJV.
10. Romans 1:20, KJV.
11. Psalm 73:28.
12. Psalm 16:2.
13. Psalm 119:37.
14. Romans 1:20.
15. 1 Timothy 2:5.
16. Romans 9:5.
17. John 14:6, KJV.
18. John 1:14.
19. Luke 1:52.
20. 1 Corinthians 1:25.
21. Genesis 3:21.
22. Romans 1:20, KJV.
23. 1 Corinthians 8:1.
24. Psalm 2:11.
25. Romans 7:22-23, RSV.
26. John 8:44.
27. Romans 7:24.
28. Proverbs 8:22.
29. Luke 23:14-15; John 14:30.
30. Colossians 2:14.
31. Psalm 51:17, RSV.

32. Revelation 21:2, RSV.
33. 2 Corinthians 1:22, NEB.
34. Psalm 116:13, KJV.
35. Psalm 62:1-2, RSV.
36. Matthew 11:28, KJV.
37. Matthew 11:29, KJV.
38. Matthew 11:25, NEB.
39. 1 Corinthians 15:9, KJV.

BOOK EIGHT · *Take Up and Read*

1. Jeremiah 33:11; Psalm 116:16-17.
2. Cf. Psalm 76:1.
3. 1 Corinthians 13:12.
4. 1 Corinthians 5:7.
5. As Augustine indicates, Simplicianus also played important roles in the conversions of Victorinus and Ambrose. He was later elected Bishop of Milan and died in 400.
6. 1 Corinthians 7:8.
7. The books Augustine read were chiefly the writings of Plotinus (205-270) and his pupil, Porphyry (232-303).
8. Cf. Colossians 2:8.
9. Matthew 11:25.
10. Ephesians 1:6.
11. Psalm 144:5, NEB.
12. Luke 12:9.
13. Luke 15:7, RSV.
14. Julian, known as the Apostate, actually reigned as emperor only from 361 to 363.
15. Cf. Galatians 5:17, KJV.
16. Ephesians 5:14, RSV.
17. Romans 7:22-23, NEB.
18. Romans 7:24-25, NEB.
19. Psalm 19:14.

20. Anthony (251?-356) was an Egyptian Christian who at about eighteen years of age gave away his possessions and devoted himself to an ascetic life, retiring to the desert in 285. He came out of solitude to organize his disciples under a rule of living, and is considered the founder of the monastic movement in the Western church.

21. Trier, or Trèves, on the river Moselle in Alsace, was an important city in the ancient Roman Empire.

22. Luke 14:28-30.

23. Matthew 11:12.

24. Cf. Romans 7:17.

25. Cf. Psalm 6:3; 51:17; 79:5,8.

26. The letters of the Apostle Paul referred to above, p. 110.

27. Cf. Matthew 19:21, KJV.

28. Romans 13:13-14, RSV.

29. Romans 14:1, RSV.

30. Ephesians 3:20, RSV.

31. See pp. 46-48.

32. Psalm 30:11.

BOOK NINE · *Genius Afire*

1. Matthew 11:30; Psalm 19:14.

2. Psalm 19:6.

3. Psalm 4:2, NEB.

4. Ephesians 1:20.

BOOK TEN · *What Is My God?*

1. 1 Corinthians 13:12.

2. Ephesians 5:27.

3. Psalm 51:6; John 3:21.

4. 1 Corinthians 2:11, Knox.

5. 1 Corinthians 13:7.

6. 2 Corinthians 12:10.

7. Romans 1:20.

8. Ephesians 2:2.

9. 2 Corinthians 11:14.

10. Romans 6:23.

11. 1 Timothy 2:5.

12. Romans 8:32.

13. Philippians 2:6-7.

14. Psalm 88:5.

15. John 10:18.

16. Hebrews 7:27.

17. John 1:14.

18. 2 Corinthians 5:15.

19. 1 Peter 5:7.

20. Cf. Psalm 119:18.

21. Colossians 2:3.

22. That is, in the fellowship of the church.

23. Psalm 22:26.

Index